HOW TO Quit Your SMOKING Habit

Without The Stress or Weight Gain

S.J. SCOTT & JONATHAN GREEN

ISBN-13: 978-1-946159-11-3

Disclaimer

Contents

Go to **www.developgoodhabits.com/smokingnotes**
for references and other notes available for this book.

Coughing Up Blood

Coughing racked my body ...

I was doubled over the sink, losing control of my body. My vision began to turn black at the edges, slowly shrinking until I could only see two pinpoints and the sink in front of me.

When the coughing subsided and I looked down, there was blood in the sink, and more than just a little. As I gazed into the mirror, my bloodshot eyes focused on the scene over my shoulder. I could see my two-year-old daughter staring at me and wondering what's wrong with Daddy.

For her entire life, and long before she came around, I had been a smoker. Her entire definition of me as a person was someone who smoked a cigarette to start my day, a cigarette after every meal, and of course, a cigarette for every break throughout the day.

As I looked at my daughter's trembling lip in the mirror, I realized something had to change.

I'd tried quitting in the past with loads of different techniques. Some of the times I quit, it lasted for months or even a year. For most of my twenties, I didn't even feel like a smoker—just someone who enjoyed the occasional smoke when he wanted to, or someone who could smoke whenever he felt like it without the risk of becoming addicted.

For so long, I was the one with all the power over smoking. But that morning, I realized something had changed. The power had shifted from me to the cigarettes. And as I looked into my daughter's terrified eyes, I realized, *This is it. Today is the day. If I don't quit now, I never will.* And even worse, I realized that if this quit failed, I would never quit again.

My grandmother died in a hospital bed with a cigarette in her hand. My uncle died in his early sixties because he couldn't quit the habit. Every night, he had to sleep with an oxygen machine that would keep him alive. Every day, as soon as his wife turned her head, he would sneak outside to have just one more cigarette. He knew they were killing him, and yet he could not stop.

Smoking was a curse within my bloodline, and it's the last thing I'd want to pass on to my sweet little daughter.

Does this story hit close to home?

If so, then let's talk about the reality of what it's like to be a smoker *and* the long-term ramifications of continuing this bad habit.

Why It's Hard to Be a Smoker

More and more in our society, smoking turns you into a pariah. People almost look at you like you're a monster when you pull a cigarette out of your pocket or ask for a lighter.

You're not allowed to smoke in bars. You're usually not allowed to smoke in hotels. You're not allowed to smoke in your own apartment building, and soon, you probably won't be allowed to smoke inside your own home.

If the public shaming and dirty looks aren't enough, smoking also breaks down your body one cell at a time. It could destroy your health, it took away several family members from me. The "beauty" of smoking is that it can affect you in so many different ways. It's a root cause leading to hypertension, lung cancer, heart problems, and even erectile dysfunction. Unlike a professional boxer, smoking isn't afraid to hit you below the belt.

We all hear stories about the friend of a friend who has a relative who lived to a hundred and ten, smoking a pack a day. But let's stop lying to ourselves and to each other: we all know that's the exception, not the rule. Despite the billions of dollars tobacco companies have spent fighting and denying that there is a correlation between ill health and cigarettes; we know there is.

If you're reading this book, there is no doubt in your mind that there are negative effects on your health from smoking, and that's just the beginning.

You also smell terrible when you smoke. The only person who doesn't realize how bad they smell when they smoke is the smoker. Only after finally setting down my cigarette that morning, after staring into my daughter's terrified eyes, did I begin to realize just how bad my stuff smelled. First, it just affects your breath. Then it's your clothing. And after smoking a long time, all of your clothes smell like smoker's clothing.

If you've ever gone to buy a used car, you can tell right away when they're trying to hide the fact that a smoker owned that car. But no matter how much they cover it with deodorizers, incense, sprays, and chemicals, you can still tell, and it puts you off. Every place we smoke eventually ends up smelling terrible, and we carry that terrible smell everywhere we go.

When I was young, restaurants used to have smoking and non-smoking sections with no barrier in between—just one side of the room and the other, as though the air wouldn't mix. When you're eating something, and the person behind you is smoking, it can ruin your meal. Because of this, we've shifted our society. As we have become more aware of the dangers of smoking and how bad it is for your health, we've increased the taxes on cigarettes in many states, and we've established more rules about where you're allowed to smoke. You're no longer allowed to smoke in most public places today.

Finally, and most importantly, smoking can cause a feeling of powerlessness. Everyone says, "I could quit smoking whenever I feel like it. I just don't want to." But then there comes that moment. The first time you decide, *You know what? I don't feel like smoking. I'm going to quit for a little while*, and you discover that you can't. You realize that this monster that's poisoning you and making you smell so gross is not so easy to shake.

That feeling of powerlessness is the worst feeling of all. It's like you're no longer in control of your behavior, your destiny, how you feel, and what you do. That can be devastating.

How to Quit the Smoking Habit

For all the reasons I just listed and so many more, **I'd like to talk about what it takes to quit the smoking habit.**

One of the struggles we face when trying to quit smoking is that we're left with a sense of emptiness. We feel like we have a hole in our lives. The more frequently you smoke, the more triggers you have that activate your desire to smoke, and the harder it can be to quit.

Our brains are not very good at quitting activities, but we're very good at picking up new habits. As I'm going to share with you throughout this book, instead of just trying to quit smoking, we're going to replace your bad habits with good ones. That way, you never suffer from that feeling of emptiness. You never face the consequence of putting on an extra ten pounds when you try to quit, replacing one health problem with another. Instead, your overall condition will improve as your sense of self improves.

We're going to take advantage of how good your body is at forming new habits and use that to fight against the desire to smoke in a way you've never experienced before. The part of your brain that's in charge of quitting habits is very weak and can easily be distracted, but the part of your brain that forms habits is incredibly strong because this is how your body increases efficiency. It turns a group of tasks into a single task, memorizes that process, and saves it into your background memory.

That's where we're going to win the war against smoking. We're going to start by changing something critical. The reason most people fail with quitting, and the reason you've probably failed in the past, is very simple. You were trying to stop doing something you wanted to do.

Every time I tried to quit smoking in the past, part of me wanted to continue. While 80 percent of me wanted to stop, 20 percent of me still missed that feeling, that sound, that ritual, that first hit of nicotine into the bloodstream. That is exactly what stops us.

I'm going to teach you how to replace your desire for smoking with a feeling of disgust. For me now, smoking is a wretched and disgusting habit. When I see people smoking, I think it's gross. I don't look at that cigarette with longing, and that's why it's been so easy for me to resist any desire to ever go back to becoming a smoker.

Your Life *After* You Quit

The most beautiful thing about putting down a cigarette is that your life begins to change immediately. Within fifteen minutes, you will experience the first health benefits.

It's a process that can take time, but you'll notice yourself getting stronger, faster, and more comfortable with your body. Breathing becomes a little easier. Unfortunately, it's a lengthy process to get back to full and complete health. It can take up to fifteen years to fully recover from however long you've been smoking. **That's why it's so critical that we start as *soon as possible*, but please realize you're not alone**.

In 2015, the CDC ran a survey and discovered that 68 percent of smokers wanted to quit. That means if you're in a room smoking with nine other people, seven out of the ten of you want to quit. That's the majority, and yet, because we don't say anything out loud, we think everyone wants to keep smoking.

Imagine "Future You"

I'd like you to take a moment and imagine what your future could be like.

What would it be like to be a non-smoker? What's it like to no longer have something in control of how you feel and how you behave? What's it like to no longer feel like a slave to a habit that you hate? What's it like to feel your life extending? Now instead of wondering if you're going to cut down in your fifties or sixties, you wonder if you're going to live to be a hundred or a hundred and twenty.

All that money you used to spend on cigarettes and cigarette taxes can now go to other positive habits and hobbies, such as movie tickets or even paying for your kids to go to college. When you look at the numbers, it can become astounding how much we spend on smoking every year.

Imagine getting up every morning, no more coughing, no more need to light up that cigarette, no more trying not to smoke in your car so you don't hurt the resale value. Suddenly, you get up and it's a brighter day. You're not out of breath. When you walk down the staircase, you feel strong and vibrant, and you're excited to grab life by the horns. You feel a sense of freedom that's been missing for so long.

Welcome to *How to Quit Your Smoking Habit*

In the following book, you will discover the excitement of leaving smoking behind. If you apply the information I'm about to teach, you will discover a variety of amazing benefits along the way:

1. **Save money.** No more spending money funding companies that don't care about you, that are selling a product they know is slowly killing you.

2. **Take control of your health.** No more getting dirty looks from your doctor or being afraid to go in for your yearly physical, but instead just feeling comfortable and confident with your body.

3. **Quit smoking without the fear of gaining weight.** You will be able to remove and replace one negative habit without replacing it with another negative habit.

4. **Stop feeling like a slave.** You will no longer feel like someone or something else is controlling your daily decisions. Smoking because you have to or because you're addicted means that the cigarettes and the tobacco are in control of you. Breaking those chains is amazingly freeing.

5. **Improve your physical fitness.** You will be able to run again and walk up a flight of stairs without breathing heavily.

6. **Become attractive again.** No more yellow teeth. No more looking old and smelling like musty nicotine.

7. **Improve your social status.** People will no longer look at you in a negative light. Kids will no longer point to you in **front** of their parents.

Do these benefits sound like something you want to experience in your life? If that's the case, then let's talk about this book and how it can assist you on your journey to breaking the smoking habit.

About *How to Quit Your Smoking Habit*

This book is part of a series titled "Develop Good Habits," which is a collaboration between myself (Jonathan Green) and Steve "S.J." Scott.

Steve is a habit master—someone who has a lot of experience helping others build (and break) habits. As he's never dealt with this form of addiction, he's fortunate enough to never have held a cigarette between his fingers. Steve and I decided to team up by using a combination of his habit framework and my personal, practical experience with quitting the smoking habit.

Together we hope to help you transform your life. We'll share stories from our lives and our expertise in dealing with different problems. Through our passion for helping people lead better lives, we will also open up and share stories from our own experience.

This book is about efficiency, and we know you have a very busy life, so these pages are not going to be filled with a lot of fluff or feel-good promises. Instead, we focus on giving you critical information in the most efficient manner possible. The goal here is to simplify the process and help you get started on the path to eliminating smoking from your life.

Furthermore, many books provide a lot of gold nuggets to improve one area of your life, but not many tell you how to build it as a specific habit into your life. They focus on theory and why, but not the *how*, and the mechanics of quitting smoking are so critical.

13

It's the little steps in between the big ideas that separate those who succeed from those who fall short.

We're going to provide you with a step-by-step framework for how to improve your life and create a long-lasting result with the minimum amount of time. Our goal is to help you replace the smoking habit in the swiftest and most painless way possible.

Some of the material in this book will be repeated in others in the series, and that's by necessity. What we've learned is that almost all habits follow similar and repeatable steps, so we feel it's important to provide a framework that you can use to build or break *any* habit.

Well, that's enough talk.

Now it's time for a little action, so let's dig into it and go from talking about ending your smoking addiction, to actually doing it.

Reflection Questions

1. Why did you pick up this book?
2. Why did you start smoking in the first place?
3. What is the main thing keeping the cigarettes in your hand?
4. Are you ready to quit, or are you on the fence?
5. Are you ready to go from 80 percent wanting to quit to 100 percent wanting to quit?
6. How does a life free of the costs and curses of cigarettes make you feel inside?

Your Action Plan

One of the best ways to accelerate your success in developing a new habit or modifying your behavior is to track your progress. Write down your experience in a notebook. This doesn't have to be anything special. It could be a notebook that you buy at the local dollar store. On the cover, write "Quit Smoking Journal."

The first thing you're going to do is answer those reflection questions from above in your journal. Next, write down the story of your life one year from now. Describe what it's like to wake up in the morning and walk outside without the need or even the desire for cigarettes.

The more detail you use to paint this picture, the better.

How do people treat you differently? How do you feel differently? How is your experience different?

Describe how amazing your life is going to be when you're no longer a smoker. Then join me in the next chapter, and we're going to take you one step closer to making that dream a reality.

The Health and Psychological Benefits of Quitting Smoking

As the CDC states, smoking is behind loads of different diseases and ailments that will shorten your lifespan and decrease the quality of your life. Here are a few things to remember about nicotine dependence:

- Most smokers become addicted to nicotine, a drug that is found naturally in tobacco.

- More people in the United States are addicted to nicotine than to any other drug.

- Research suggests that nicotine may be as addictive as heroin, cocaine, or alcohol.

- Quitting smoking is hard and may require several attempts.

- People who stop smoking often start again because of withdrawal symptoms, stress, and weight gain.

Nicotine withdrawal symptoms may include:

- Feeling irritable, angry, or anxious

- Having trouble thinking

- Craving tobacco products

- Feeling hungrier than usual

Fortunately, there is also some good news about nicotine dependence. Quitting smoking is associated with the following health benefits:

- Lowered risk for many types of cancer, including lung cancer

- Reduced risk for heart disease, stroke, and peripheral vascular disease (narrowing of the blood vessels outside your heart)

- Reduced risk of heart disease within one to two years of quitting

- Reduced respiratory symptoms, such as coughing, wheezing, and shortness of breath. While these symptoms may not disappear, they do not continue to progress at the same rate among people who quit, compared with those who continue to smoke.

- Reduced risk of developing some lung diseases (such as chronic obstructive pulmonary disease, also known as COPD, one of the leading causes of death in the United States).

- Reduced risk for infertility in women of childbearing age. Women who stop smoking during pregnancy also reduce their risk of having a low birth weight baby.

The Real-World Benefits of Quitting Smoking

The above bullet points and factoids don't paint the full picture of what it's like to stop smoking. Let's talk about what *you* will experience when you break this habit.

Here are a few immediate benefits you'll experience:

- Within twenty minutes of setting down your final cigarette, your heart rate drops to normal level.

- Within just twelve hours, the carbon monoxide level within your bloodstream drops to a normal level.

- As early as just two weeks later, your risk of having a heart attack begins to drop, and your lung function begins to improve.

- Over the course of the first nine months, your coughing and shortness of breath will begin to decrease. Each breath you take will be fuller and more pleasant. You'll be almost shocked by how much oxygen you can actually bring into your bloodstream a year after quitting.

That's how fast you can start to experience amazing results.

Within five to fifteen years, your risk of having a stroke becomes that of someone who's never smoked a day in their life, and your risk of getting cancer (especially mouth, throat, and esophagus) is half that of a smoker.

Ten years after quitting, your risk of dying from lung, bladder, cervical, or pancreatic cancer is slashed in half compared to when you were smoking.

And finally, fifteen years after quitting, your risk of a heart attack is exactly the same place it would be if you had never smoked.

Beyond these long-term benefits, and I know sometimes it's hard to look at how I'm going feel in fifteen years, there are some amazing additional benefits:

#1: Quality of life. When I was a chronic smoker, I needed a cigarette just to get back to normal. I always felt a step behind. I got sick all the time. I've had pneumonia and bronchitis nearly twenty times in my life; since I stopped smoking, I haven't had either—not once.

I remember one day, as I was walking out the front door, I realized I had forgotten something in our bedroom on the top floor. I said, "You know what? Forget it. You might as well be on the other side of a mountain. It's too far away," which is crazy, because in high school I used to skip one or even two steps going up and down the stairs between class. But now the thought of trudging up and down a staircase turned into a nightmare.

Feeling better is one of the greatest benefits of quitting. You no longer feel like your body is edging closer and closer to death. Instead, you can feel more vibrant even as you enter your thirties, forties, and fifties. It's like regaining part of your youth.

#2: Health. Beyond just feeling better, you will actually *be* better. Since ending my addiction to nicotine, I go to the doctor less often. In the last year, every single member of my family has had to go to the hospital except me. I'm older than my wife and children, and yet I'm the one in the best health. It feels amazing to go to the dentist without fear of the dentist gagging at the smell coming out of my mouth. It feels great to go to the doctor's office without wondering if my blood pressure is going to be so high they want to put me on a treacherous medication.

#3: The smell. The first thing I noticed after I quit smoking was how disgusting certain parts of my house and the clothes that I hadn't washed yet smelled. When you smoke, you're the only one who can't smell how bad it is. When you quit, you realize just how disgusting you smell and taste. I don't know how my wife put up with kissing me when I tasted like an ashtray. Now she doesn't have to suffer from that anymore.

#4: The cost. Cigarettes can cost anywhere from $5 to $15 in some places. That really adds up over time.

Do the math: If you're smoking just a pack a day, you will spend a minimum of $35 a week. If you're at the bottom end of the price spectrum, that's $120 a month or around $1,500 a year. What could you do with an extra $1,500 in your pocket? Right now, I'm able to take my family to the movies every single week and know that the price of those tickets (and even some snacks) is less than my smoking habit, and it's much more pleasurable.

#5: A proud family. My wife and child were horrified, watching me smoke and cough up blood. Not only were we spending money on cigarettes, but we were having to spend more money on medication and hospital bills. It was all adding up. Now they're proud of me. They couldn't be more excited that, not only did I conquer my smoking demon, but I am now someone who teaches other people the same path.

#6: Skin. I always remember that old *Seinfeld* episode where Kramer decided to turn his apartment into a smoker's apartment because the smokers weren't allowed to smoke anywhere else, and within just a few weeks, his skin had turned to leather. A little bit of an exaggeration, but it's also true.

Even before you smell someone, take a look at their hands and skin, and you know they're a smoker. Their fingers have that yellowish nicotine soot, and their skin is an unhealthy, sallow color. After I quit smoking, I was amazed to find out people thought I was ten years younger.

#7: Living longer and seeing your kids grow up. This is honestly the biggest benefit for me. The thought of not seeing my daughter graduate high school, start her career, or fall in love terrifies me. Knowing that I've turned the odds in my favor makes me very happy. I feel confident I'll be there to see my grandkids and, hopefully, even my great-grand-kids. Believe me, I wish my grandmother were here to meet my kids. I wish my uncle, who I was very close with, was here to meet my kids and visit me. It makes me sad to think about him missing out on that, let alone missing out on meeting his own grandkids. That's a tragedy that my kids won't have to suffer because of cigarettes anymore.

#8: No more public judgment. It's come full circle. Before, people would look at me like I was a monster, and now I look at smokers in the same way. Not because I hate them, but because looking at smoking as disgusting helps me avoid temptation. I don't have to fight the desire to smoke. I've killed that desire.

#9: You don't feel like a slave anymore. I remember one of my close friends in college couldn't get out of bed without having a cigarette. He used to leave an ashtray right next to his mattress, and he would lie back in bed, light up a cigarette, and smoke it directly over his pillow. That's how little control he had over himself. He could not function without his morning cigarette.

I know what it's like to feel powerless. I remember wanting to quit so many times. I'd have half a pack of cigarettes and go, "Oh, I don't want these to go to waste," and I'd always try and quit between packs, but I couldn't. Now I can make all my own decisions again. I feel a sense of freedom that I missed for so long.

#10: Sports and fitness. At my worst point, I looked in the mirror and said to myself, "Well, Jonathan, you'll never be able to get up a flight of stairs without your heart racing and huffing and puffing like the wolf from 'The Three Little Pigs.' You're never going to run again, and you have to accept that your feet are attached to the ground. You'll never jump again." I was in my early thirties, and I had already given up three of the biggest parts of my life.

Five years later, I practice kickboxing five days a week with a professional fighter. I'm jumping, spinning kicks, throwing elbows, running, and doing jumping jacks and push-ups. I do it all. Everything I do on a daily basis used to be on my forgotten list. It feels amazing to do all the things I enjoyed in high school, to be able to say, "I don't have to let go of those things."

It doesn't matter if you're fifty, sixty, or seventy. When you set down that pack of smokes, you can start recapturing new health and fitness territory. You can start walking faster, and then jogging, and riding a bicycle becomes a possibility again.

#11: It's easier to breathe. It's not just your imagination. When you quit smoking, over that first year, your lungs will clear up, and your body will become more efficient. You'll take in larger amounts of air and therefore, convert a larger percentage of oxygen with every breath. I know what it's like to feel short of breath, but now it's only a memory. I can jog, run, sprint, and breathing is never a limitation. My lungs used to tie me to the ground, but now they've become my wings.

#12: More energy. Unfortunately, in our society, we think the answer to every problem is a chemical.

Trouble waking up in the morning? Drink a cup of coffee.

Feeling down in the dumps? Smoke a cigarette.

Feeling lonely? Drink some alcohol.

And that's before we even get into over-the-counter prescription medication. I used to think that energy came from chemicals. Drinking sketchy energy drinks and smoking cigarettes was how I powered through my long work sessions, writing my first books and building my business. But now that I don't smoke, I never run out of energy. I wake up every morning between 4:00 and 5:00 a.m., not because I set an alarm but because my body is always ready to kick-start the day.

You'll be amazed at how much energy is unlocked when you can fully access your lungs, and your blood begins to pump oxygen-filled hemoglobin through your body at maximum efficiency. See, we're accustomed to using cigarettes and other chemicals to fill the gap, but all we're doing is swapping one problem with another. If you just get rid of that original problem, you'll discover there's an amazing amount of energy waiting within your body, ready to be unlocked.

#13: Lower stress. The irony of cigarettes is that we often think of them as a stress reliever. This was one of the most common responses we received when Steve and I polled our audiences: we need cigarettes to lower stress. But in fact, cigarettes are the opposite. They only create a placebo effect.

The main measure of stress is blood pressure, and smoking raises your blood pressure. Since I've quit smoking, I've only had one blood pressure scare. I was getting a physical three years ago. My blood pressure was so high that they wanted to put me on very powerful medication. I said, "Before you do that, let's run this test again." The second time they ran the tests, I closed my eyes. I relaxed myself, and

I got a perfect score. Just to be on the safe side, I bought a little blood pressure machine from the pharmacy near my house. I test myself at least once a week, and in the past two years, my blood pressure has been rock solid. The number one indicator of stress says that I'm doing pretty good.

#14: You're better in the bedroom. Nicotine, high blood pressure, and problems in your bloodstream due to smoking are one of the primary causes of erectile dysfunction. Let me just tell you that when you quit smoking, whether you're a man or a woman, your performance in the bedroom will improve.

#15: Fertility. Every time my wife and I decided to have a new child since I quit smoking, she got pregnant the first day we tried. If that's not fertility, I don't know what it is.

#16: Eliminate secondhand smoke. Because I had a young child at the time, when I was smoking the most, I had to go outside and smoke on a tiny ledge outside the window. Among my friends from high school, the ones whose parents smoked are those with the biggest smoking problems now. Whether or not you believe all those commercials from the nineties about secondhand smoke and its dangerous effects, I can tell you that when your parents smoke, it affects you. It certainly makes you more likely to pick up smoking yourself. I don't want that for my kids.

#17: Cholesterol. Smoking is a precursor for loads of diseases. Not only does it increase your blood pressure, but it also increases your cholesterol and causes blockages in your bloodstream. There's a reason science points to such a tight correlation between smoking and heart attacks. The good news is that when you quit smoking, your risk of heart attack decreases immediately, and your cholesterol begins to normalize as well.

#18: Thin blood and the danger of blood clots. In addition to everything else, it turns out that smoking puts you at risk for throwing a blood clot, which can go to your heart, brain, or lungs and kill you. As if smoking couldn't kill you in enough different ways.

#19: Hypertension. *Hypertension* is just another cool name for high blood pressure. If you look at the ten most common causes of death for Americans, six of them are caused by hypertension. Smoking doesn't kill you directly. It'll give you hypertension and shatter you another way.

In addition to these amazing benefits, when you quit smoking, it helps to prevent hearing and vision loss. You get stronger bones, muscles, and immune system, and you even heal from wounds more quickly.

The Dangers of Inaction

We just talked about the many health benefits of quitting smoking. Now let me briefly describe what it's like to fall into the trap of *inaction*.

I live on the beach. In fact, I'm standing on a dock right now, dictating this chapter while the waves roll in. The beach teaches us a valuable lesson. If I stand in the sand with my feet in the water, and my feet don't move, I do not hold still. Each time the waves come in and crash against my feet, they pull me a little deeper into the ocean. If I stand still long enough, eventually, I'll get pulled all the way out to sea and end up in the middle of the ocean.

Inaction is not standing still. Just because you're not taking action right now doesn't mean nothing's happening. Every day you put off replacing the smoking habit, your condition is getting a little bit worse, and you're one step further from success.

Each time you say, "Not yet," or, "I'm not ready," or, "I can't do it," you push yourself a little further away from success. The longer you fail to act, the lower your faith in yourself becomes, and eventually, you will stop believing that you have any willpower at all.

Additionally, your health continues to deteriorate. Each cigarette takes a few minutes off your lifespan, and you know it. You're not reading this book because you wonder if smoking is bad for you. You're reading this book because you want someone to motivate you and give you a path to breaking free.

The final and most devastating effect of inaction is that you might pass this on to your children. If you think people look negatively at you now when you smoke, imagine how people will look at your kids in twenty or thirty years when they're the ones left smoking.

We've talked a great deal about the benefits of quitting and the power of leaving smoking behind, not because you need to know this list but because I want to motivate you into getting excited to quit. Having all these different reasons in front of you helps get you pumped up and ready.

It's time to go from thinking to acting. This book isn't just about stopping smoking. This book is an action guide. It's a series of steps that you're going to implement with the result and the benefit that smoking will exit your life.

Reflection Questions

1. Which of the health benefits from the CDC can you most connect to? Are you excited about how you'll feel in fifteen minutes, a year, or fifteen years?

2. Which of the benefits from the extensive list and the stories I've shared from my life most resonates with you?

3. Were any of these benefits surprising to you, or were you unaware of them?

4. Which of the problems I've described do you already suffer from? Have you had a wound that wouldn't heal? Have you had problems with your lungs? Have you been sick often? Did someone make a bad comment about your skin?

5. Are you excited now to be on this journey with us and to be cooperating with someone who's been where you are, someone who knows what it's like and has broken free?

Your Action Plan

Choose the most important benefit, the one that resonates with you the most, and create a vision board. Find pictures and put them onto a piece of poster board. You're going to create a vision for your future where that benefit is going to be your life.

This poster board is going to become your motivation. It's your vision for *your* future, and I want you to put it somewhere you'll see it all the time.

Tape it to the ceiling above your bed, so it's the last thing you see at night and the first thing you see in the morning to remind you of why you're going through this process.

Even though you'll have short-term twinges at times, you can look at that board and go, "No, that's the life I want. That's the future I want!"

Spend some time on building your vision board. When it's ready and you've hung it on the wall, join me in the next chapter.

What Is the "Right" Way to Quit Smoking?

Before we dive into the step-by-step process of the book, let's take a moment to talk about the most popular techniques that people use to quit smoking. To be honest, each has its pros and cons, which is why we've incorporated more than one approach into our habit framework.

Let's review five of the most popular ways to stop smoking:

#1: Going "cold turkey" and using willpower alone.

You stop smoking in an instant. You throw out any remaining cigarettes and decide from that moment forward never to smoke again. The moment you quit is clearly defined.

Pros:

- you can start immediately
- no slow weaning-off period
- clear date when you quit smoking
- you can start it today
- it doesn't cost anything

Cons:

- struggle with physical and psychological addiction
- just one slip up with a cigarette can cause this method to break
- very brittle
- when you make a mistake with this method, you blame yourself, and it can make it harder to try again.

#2: Using nicotine tools like gum, the patch, or similar devices.

This is a slower approach that gives you time to deal with the cravings. First, you replace your cigarettes with an alternative containing nicotine, and over time, you wean yourself off with smaller and smaller doses of nicotine.

Pros:

- helps you deal with both the chemical and psychological addiction separately
- weans you off slowly from the physical addiction to nicotine
- separates the physical addiction from the act of smoking
- scientifically designed to be very effective

Cons:

- can be quite expensive
- leaves you still addicted to the high of nicotine, even if you leave smoking behind.

#3: Leveraging a powerful support network.

Join a support group or surround yourself with other quitters to help you stay the course. Similar to the effects of joining Alcoholics Anonymous.

Pros:

- people there to stand by your side
- never feel like you're alone
- quitting is treated like a process
- it takes the pressure off your shoulders and decreases the risk of self-blame

Cons:

- your support network isn't always there with you
- if somebody in your support networks slips up, they can bring you down with them
- you become reliant on an external source of confidence
- you can quit without building the correct psychological infra-structure, leading to relapse

#4: Taking a prescription medication.

There are very powerful medications, such as Chantix, containing the active ingredient varenicline. It works by activating the part of your brain that enjoys nicotine and prevents nicotine from attaching to the receptors there.

Pros:

- can shut down the addiction very quickly
- very powerfully targets the addiction centers
- produces quick and effective results
- requires the involvement of a doctor
- follow a customized plan built around your current smoking addiction
- best way to get you (as an individual) free

Cons:

- expensive
- replaces one chemical dependency with another
- possible side effects that lead to additional health problems

#5. Using a vaping device.

Electronic cigarettes heat up a liquid, which may or may not contain nicotine, and create a vapor rather than smoke (think steam from boiling water).

Pros:

- you can vape in many places where smoking is prohibited
- allows you to maintain the physical habit without the addiction habit
- very quick and effective technique
- allows you to slowly wean yourself off the most dangerous chemicals in cigarettes

Cons:

- can be unbelievably expensive

- most companies are actually being purchased and swallowed up by traditional tobacco companies, so you're giving your money to the exact same company that was poisoning you in the first place

- you replace one version of smoking with another; you still have this habit that, at best, is neutral

- you're relying on technology, and if technology fails, you can crumble. If your vaping battery dies, and you need to run and buy an overpriced vaping battery, you can slip back into buying cigarettes

Now, before we move on, I want to dedicate a separate section here to the potential dangers of vaping; it's such a new habit that no one knows what the long-term effects of vaping are. It may turn out that vaping is just as bad or even worse than smoking, so I do list it here as a temporary replacement for smoking, but I do not recommend it for continued use.

The FDA has been taking significant steps to protect Americans from dangers of tobacco through new regulation, and the new rules include e-cigarettes as well. Vaping is classified as addictive, and it is not allowed under eighteen years of age.

Some of the side effects that have been observed due to vaping include:

- Dry mouth

- Sore mouth

- Dizziness

- Cough

- Dry skin

- Itchiness

- Dry eyes

- Nosebleeds

- Bleeding gums

- Headache

- Tongue inflammation

- Black tongue

- Sleepiness

- Sleeplessness

- Allergies

- Chest pain

- Breathing problems

Even though it is called "vaping," only a small proportion of what you're inhaling is actually water vapor. Mostly, it's propylene glycol, and previous research showed it can cause eye and lung irritation. In its product safety assessment for propylene glycol, the Dow Chemical Company recommends individuals avoid inhaling the chemical.

A new study by Goniewicz and colleagues in *Nicotine & Tobacco Research* reveals that potentially toxic carbonyls can form when e-liquids are heated to high temperatures, with levels of carcinogenic formaldehyde observed in the range seen in tobacco smoke. Last but not least, some of the flavorings in e-cigarettes can be toxic.

How to Build the Right Plan for You

Most quit-smoking plans, strategies, tactics, and methods are built around the idea of eliminating the smoking habit. The reason vaping is the most popular (and right now, most people find it the best and most effective method) is that it uses replacement ideology, replacing the bad habit with a better one.

If none of the methods above seems like the right fit for you, don't be scared to try something more unusual. Do some research, ask other people who managed to quit, join a Facebook group (like ours: www.habitsgroup.com), and ask other members what methods they are trying. Some people found success with more unconventional strategies, such as hypnosis, self-talk, Pilates, or even laser therapy, but they were able to quit, and that's all that matters.

One of our readers shared that he had tried everything, but nothing worked. He was so desperate that he joined a program offered by the Seventh-day Adventist Church (despite not being a member). After five days of seminars, where they illustrated some very specific tools—such as cold mitten friction technique, having a buddy, and changing where you usually sit, among other ideas)—he quit and has not smoked since.

Our focus going forward is to use the techniques that work best for you as part of an overall plan to build up a healthy lifestyle, *one small habit at a time.*

Looking at the pros and cons of the common alternatives listed above, you may be willing to use some and not others. Our goal is to get to a place where you aren't relying on any of these habits—whether it's gum, vaping, or patches—to stand between you and your addiction.

Instead, we're going to fully replace that habit. You'll be on the path to success, and the desire to smoke will disappear. We're going to eliminate the temptation at the root so that you don't have to struggle through this process; instead, you'll find it's shockingly easy on both an emotional and an implementational level.

Take a look through this list and see which of these methods you're comfortable with and which you are not. Studies by the CDC have shown that combining methodologies is the most effective approach. Combining willpower with emotional support and the involvement of a medical professional can be the triumvirate of success when you're deep down the path of addiction.

There is no one perfect solution that works for everyone. Instead, we're going to give you a framework that you can tailor to your personal situation.

Reflection Questions

1. Which of these methods have you tried in the past and failed?

2. What's your main hurdle to quitting?

3. What's your biggest fear about the process of quitting?

4. Looking at each of these methods, what do you think is the biggest con?

5. Why do these methods fail for so many people while they work for a select few?

Your Action Plan

As we move into the action phase of this book, we're going to really focus on implementation, because now the ball's in your court. To get started, we're going to do something together.

It's called "the one-day quit."

Simply put: you're going to stop smoking, cold turkey for twenty-four hours.

That means tomorrow morning when you wake up, you know you're not going to have another cigarette until after you sleep again. You're just going to go through a twenty-four-hour stop-smoking cycle, and then we're going to analyze every step in the process. As you go through this, you'll journal your entire experience.

Some people really need a cigarette first thing in the morning. Others need it right after a meal, when something stressful happens, or during the drive to work. We want to make a list and develop a detailed plan built around your habits, so we know each of your smoking triggers. We'll use this list later to continue customizing our habit stacking plan to replace your smoking habit.

Remember: this is only the first step in the process, *not* the entire process.

If you slip up and have a cigarette at lunchtime, try to go the rest of the day without smoking. Rank each time you have a craving or trigger and rate how hard it is on a scale of one to ten. If you slip up and have a cigarette, that's obviously a ten. The desire was so powerful that it broke through your willpower. That's OK. We're going to find and isolate those most powerful triggers and attack them first as we build through this process.

Spend enough time writing in your journal and getting to know yourself. When you spend a day without smoking, you'll discover triggers that you didn't even realize were there. Once you've completed this process, join me in the next chapter.

STEP 1

Connect to Your Purpose

Nobody quits smoking without a reason why.

I want to be very vulnerable with you here about my entire experience in the arc of my "smoking career." I had my first cigarette when I was around fifteen, and my last cigarette in my early thirties. Unlike many people who quit, I can't tell you the exact day. I don't have it on my calendar. All I know is it was a Sunday in August, three to four years ago.

During my time as a smoker, I had time on and time off, and I didn't become a heavy smoker until my late twenties. At that time, part of the reason I smoked was that all the cute girls were smoking. I discovered that hanging out in the smoking section outside of a bar or club, where everyone was forced to congregate, made it very easy to start conversations.

At first, I would just have a lighter in my pocket and hang out, but then, I became the person who always had a pack of smokes. My addiction slipped into overdrive. After I no longer went to bars and clubs or needed to meet new people, after I was married and started having children, I continued to smoke, even though the original purpose had disappeared.

I picked up smoking because I thought I looked cool. During my smoking years, I tried to quit many times for different reasons, and one of the biggest blocks for me was that whenever I would try and quit, people around me would offer me cigarettes and say, "Just quit later. Just have one, it's no big deal."

I didn't experience a lot of peer pressure, but I experienced that when you quit smoking, all your friends who are smokers start to feel a little bit lonely. You become a mirror reflecting their bad decision, and if they can keep you from quitting, it keeps their guilt from getting stronger.

What Is Your Reason *Why?*

There comes a point when you say, "I'm not going to take it anymore. I have to make a change." Until you lock down with the right purpose for you, it will be extremely hard to break this habit.

When I tried to quit smoking because I was scared by my uncle's death and I was worried about long-term health issues, it never worked. Every pack of cigarettes in the world has a warning or a picture on it of someone dying from smoking, and yet people still smoke from those packs all the time. The long-term warning doesn't work.

One of the things we'll focus on in this book is helping you build healthy habits that relate to your "core why," the specific reason why you want to quit smoking.

My core why, looking at my daughter's eyes in that moment, was the desire to be with her, to be there for her, to be a better father. That became my central tenet. Every time I tried to quit for my wife—because I wanted to give her a better life, and I wanted her to kiss someone who didn't smell disgusting—it failed to stick.

What is *your* core why?

When identifying the reason why you want to quit, it's important to know what you want from life. You only have a little time each day to make things happen, so you should focus on the tasks that give you the biggest bang for your buck. It's a simple process of knowing what truly matters to you and building a routine that supports your life.

We've gone through massive lists of benefits and talked about every area of your life, and the reason we did that first was help make this question easy for you to answer. You should choose a core goal that resonates with you the most. It doesn't have to be the same as mine. Maybe for you, the most important reason is you don't want your teeth to be gross anymore. Whichever reason resonates with you, lock into that.

Ideally, you should choose a core goal that is also short-term. Short-term goals are more powerful. When a goal is far away, we struggle to reach for it and visualize it. Very few people can set a plan that will take them fifteen years to achieve and stay the course.

When you latch onto a faraway goal, it can be very hard to stay the course because you're fighting urges daily. At first, this is about sticking to a habit you can do right now. For the first several weeks and months, when I stopped smoking, it was a daily process. If you've been through any of the anonymous programs (Alcoholics Anonymous, Narcotics Anonymous, etc.), their whole methodology is built around the idea of "one day at a time."

We want to focus on building a win each day. After you win seven days in a row, you've won a week. After you win thirty days in a row, you've won a month. That's the process we're building, but it starts by having a goal that's close enough to motivate you to win a daily battle.

Examples of Core *Whys* You Can Use

There are a number of great examples of core goals you can use. Number one is illness or the fear of illness. I was struck with more than a dozen different lung ailments and breathing problems, and it wasn't enough to make me quit. But the fear of struggling with emphysema or having to sleep with a breathing mask or an oxygen tank might be what you latch onto.

Perhaps for you, health is the best reason. You want to be faster, to run again, to recapture your youth, to be able to do a jumping jack or play dodgeball again. The desire to do the sports of your youth or participate in activities you've always missed out on can lock you in and motivate you.

Family can be another great reason. Maybe you've lost a relative or wish to connect with someone or hope to be someone's role model.

Fear works well too. If you're just afraid of dying or getting sick, that could be a very powerful motivator. Fear is a very strong emotion, and you'll find that whenever you have those moments of temptation, fear is stronger than desire. It will help you to break through and stay the course.

Finally, something as simple as stress might be your core why. Smoking is stressful, and stress is just a form of chronic or long-term daily fear. If you think about quitting smoking all the time, and it's starting to stress you out because you feel like you're trapped in a cycle, then the idea of pushing away that stress and lowering your blood pressure could be something you think about every day.

You can do what I did: Buy a blood pressure machine for around $25 and check your levels every day. You'll watch them get lower as you stop smoking, so every time you're tempted to have a cigarette, you shove your arm in that machine and push the button. Thirty seconds later, the temptation disappears because you're happy with your results.

Do I Need a *Why*?

Our Western culture has shifted over the last 100 years to instant gratification. Before the invention of credit cards last century, most Americans had a good amount of money saved away. If you wanted to buy an amazing Christmas present for your kids or family members, you would use a process called "layaway," which almost doesn't exist anymore. *Layaway* is where you pick an item and have the store set it aside. You make a small payment for weeks or months in advance, and only when you've made the final payment do you receive the item.

It's the exact opposite of a credit card. With a credit card, you receive the item and then end up paying for it later, and of course, you pay more than the original price. Nowadays, we imagine that layaway is reserved for poor people, but in fact, layaway is a far more frugal and fiscally responsible approach. Someone who uses layaway as a process to pay for something has demonstrated they have a quality that I respect a great deal because most of us don't have that quality anymore. We're so used to instant gratification.

How many people announce a diet on social media just to get that instant feeling of gratification? We want the gratification without the effort, and that's the reason we need a real *why*. The gratification, the good vibes, the high fives we'll get for quitting smoking will not last for a very long time, and they're not enough to carry us through this process.

We need an internal source of motivation, *not* an external source of validation.

Trying to quit smoking in the past has generated a broken loop. It hasn't worked for you yet. You've seen the CDC statistics. Even the majority of high school smokers have tried to quit or want to, and most adults—70 percent of us—have tried to quit in the last year. I can guarantee you that a big part of the reason many of those efforts failed was the lack of a core *why*.

Additionally, we make the common mistake of doing a habit pile instead of a habit stack. A *habit pile* is where you try to change fifty things about you at the same time. I don't want you to mistakenly think that I'm perfect. I'm not perfect in behavior, manner, relationships, or appearance. I am simply someone who's a little further up the hill than you when it comes to smoking.

My body is not perfect. As I tried to quit smoking and picked it back up several times, each time I quit smoking for a while, I fell into that common trap of gaining weight. Even after I quit smoking for good, while I didn't gain weight in the short term, I stopped paying attention, and I put on some weight. About a year later, because I was so proud of myself for quitting smoking without gaining weight, I then rewarded myself by gaining weight. I made a classic, stupid blunder.

But here's the thing. Since then, I've added in more fitness habits. My weight is continually pushing down rather than up. Do not try to add multiple habits at the same time. Don't try to lose weight and quit smoking at the same time. If you do things in order, in a linear process, you will find great success. If you try to do them all at once, it becomes too much change because your body and your mind don't reprogram that way.

There are many effective fitness habits in my life, one of which is very personal. About a year ago, I discovered I have a major problem with my eyes. It got so bad I thought I was going blind, and it terrified me. I make a living as a writer. I spend the majority of my time on the computer, and I started to freak out, thinking, *How can I support my family if I can't see?* My daughter and son rely on me; that's a great weight I carry on my shoulders.

As part of my process of discovery, I learned that there isn't a problem with my eyes. There's a problem with my eyes when I use a computer. I can't be on a computer twelve hours a day like I used to when I was writing all the time. I'm a big writer. I've written a lot of books under many different pen names, and I've even ghostwritten over a hundred different books for clients, so losing my greatest skill terrified me.

Through this process, I realized: "I need to find a way to continue supporting my family even if I lose my vision." I experimented with different methods and technologies until I shifted my approach. Now I dictate all my books. I'm always experimenting with different ways to be more efficient and to create content without having to lay eyes on a computer.

When I first started dictating, I would sit down in the restaurant in front of my house on the beach. I would watch the waves, go through my outline, and dictate. Then I switched and built a new habit. Now I walk along a thirty-foot dock over the waves, back and forth, the whole time I'm dictating. See what I did? I found a way to add in another healthy habit. Instead of sitting at a computer twelve hours a day, I walk three to four hours and get the same amount of work done.

It took me some time to build this process, but because I stacked the habits, I was able to achieve it. It's very important that you avoid the mistake of trying to fix or change multiple habits at the same time. Instead, fix one habit at a time so you're continually getting better as a person; this way, you never feel overwhelmed.

Finally, quitting smoking or starting any habit just because you "should" never works. It's not enough motivation. Unfortunately, it's pretty easy to pick up bad habits that way, but it's very hard to pick up good ones.

Recently, Steve sent out a survey to his entire audience. He asked: What was your #1 impediment to quitting smoking? What was your greatest success? And what methods have you tried in the past? We wanted to connect with our audience and make sure that this book dials into everyone's real experience.

One thing we discovered was that several people admitted they should quit but just don't feel like it. And that's OK. You might not be in a place yet where you're ready to quit, and unless you latch onto a powerful *why*, you don't really feel like it, and won't actually do it. None of us do things that we don't really feel like doing, even though we think we should. We all know we should eat perfectly clean and healthy every single day, but almost nobody does it.

Let's Find Your Core *Why* Together

We've covered lots of reasons why people want to quit and all the different benefits of doing so, but I want you to be more specific. If you can get very specific about your motivation, then you'll latch on to it more firmly.

"I want to stay healthy," is not nearly as effective as, "I don't want to die from emphysema like my uncle did," or, "I don't want to have to sleep with a COPD machine over my face every night looking like Darth Vader so that my son is afraid of me at night and doesn't want to sleep in the same room as me."

My core *why* was, "I don't want to leave my daughter in this world alone before it's my time. I don't want to lose a single day with her." That *why* is so important to me that even though I'm out here on my dock dictating this book, she is fifty yards away from me, training with our kickboxing instructor, and I can see her. That's how important my personal *why* is.

There are loads of *whys* that can connect with you. How about, "I'd like to take the amount of money I spend on smoking every year and use it to buy a new car or go on vacation instead." Pick something specific; save up for something you want.

Reflection Questions

1. Look at each of the different categories of benefits to quitting smoking and see which ones resonate with you the most.

2. Once you've figured out which categories resonate with you the most, organize them and rank them by how long they'll take and how emotionally connected you feel to them.

3. Write down very specific statements about each of these categories, such as, "I don't want to die young," or, "I'm afraid of getting lung cancer," or, "I don't want my child to ever look me in the eyes and ask me if I'm going to die."

4. Continue this process, answering these questions until you find your *why*. It will be the answer that affects you most deeply, the one that feels visceral; it will hit you in the stomach and make you want to cry as you're writing it down. That's when you have found your why.

Your Action Plan

Continue to work through these reflection questions and dial in to finding your ultimate *why*. As part of this process, consider joining a community or our Facebook group and post questions about your experiences. You do not have to participate in this process in isolation, so your activity is to find and join a community and post your *why*.

If you haven't dial in to your *why* yet, you can ask questions in the group, read other people's *whys*, and use that community to find it. Once you have shared it within our community, write it down in your journal and add it to your vision board.

Write down your goal and make it visual. Bring it into the real world, out of your mind and onto the wall. Once you've connected with our community and created that powerful visualization, move on to Step 2 and join me in the next chapter.

STEP 2

Create a Specific Smoke-Related Goal

While we talk a great deal about goals and habits, it is important to make sure that you and I are speaking the same language, so that when I use a term our definitions are the same.

For instance: a *goal* is the broad outcome that you want to achieve in life. It's how you connect with your purpose. It's the transformation you want to experience. In this case, your goal is to never smoke again.

And a *habit* is the secret of this process. It is the day-to-day execution of that goal.

Habits aren't nearly as sexy as goals, but ultimately, it's what you do daily that determines what you're able to achieve in life. Now that we have your end goal, we have to break that apart into tiny habits you can implement throughout the day.

As you learned from your one-day quit, smoking is a series of small habits. It's a series of moments throughout the day where you decide to have or not have a cigarette. Even if you have an extreme habit and you're smoking two or three packs a day, most of the day, you're not actually smoking.

There are huge swathes of your day when you're not smoking, so you're capable of that. If you're further down the path, and your habit is continuous, then the first thing we have to do is break and replace your first-thing-in-the-morning habit. You'll discover that when you have a habit chain, if you break the beginning of that chain, the rest of the process becomes surprisingly easy, and we can stack healthy habits throughout the day to build up and support that one effective habit.

Creating Daily Health Habits

At a core level, habits are simply the day-to-day execution of a goal that's personally important, and the keyword there is "personally." It means that the goal resonates with you. That's why we have to find the right one. Now that you've completed that process and you have a vision board on your wall, you know your personal goal. We live one day at a time, and you know that short-term pleasure often beats long-term reward.

It's very important to connect the underlying reasons why you'd like to improve the area of your life, and this is the power of small actions. Take a moment and imagine what life would be like if you began each day with small actions that create a chain reaction of positive benefits throughout your life. You eat a healthy breakfast, have a great conversation with your loved ones, and then begin your workday focusing on the important tasks. Then, throughout the day, you complete other habits that positively impact your top goals. I guarantee you'd feel more fulfilled, get more accomplished, and have a better direction for your career. All of this can be possible when you focus on small actions that relate to your important goals.

These habits don't require much effort. In fact, most only take five minutes or less to complete. But they have a powerful compounding effect if you repeat them often enough.

Use the S.M.A.R.T. Goals Framework

You may have heard this term in other places. S.M.A.R.T. is a very specific way of building goals. It was first written in November 1981 in an issue of *Management Review* by George T. Doran. Let me take you through the five letters of S.M.A.R.T.

S – Specific. You want something specific that is simple, sensible, significant, and clarifies what your goal is. If our goal is "stop smoking," that's OK, but we need to be a bit more detailed. One of the mistakes people make when trying to lose weight is they don't write down a specific number. If we don't make it specific, we're hedging our bets, and we might end up quitting after a small, single victory.

That's the problem with a non-specific goal. In our case, because we're ending a habit, we can be very specific and even break it apart by saying, "I want to go from three packs a day to one pack a day." That can be our first goal, and then we can say, "I want to drop down from a pack a day to five cigarettes a day." You can progressively work your way toward zero cigarettes per day.

M – Measurable. A goal should be measurable, and that means it should have a number in it. If I say I want to lose ten pounds and I lose three, I know I'm 30 percent of the way to my goal. That's why even if your goal is to stop smoking completely, I want you to count how many cigarettes you're having a day and use that as your baseline. Now your goal is measurable.

Most of the time, we say, "I want to quit smoking," but then we have a single cigarette and feel like a total failure. That's because our goals are brittle, and our efforts to quit can shatter in that moment. You're more likely to succeed by having a measurable goal.

A – Attainable or Achievable. This is a goal that you can realistically reach during this cycle. If you're smoking three or five packs a day, jumping from that to zero in a single day is too much. We want to create a time line that's effective for you. During this process, you may have to shift your goals forward or back a little bit. You may initially say it will take you three months, but it turns out it will take five. That's not quitting; that's adapting. On the other hand, you may also discover that you're ahead of schedule.

R – Relevant or Reasonable. We want a goal that connects with our *why*. You're already there, of course, because this is a book about a single type of goal, and every *why* we've shared is directly connected to that. I believe you're already in the right zone for relevant.

T – Time-Sensitive. This is the most important part for me. As long as your goal is specific, measurable, and time-sensitive, you've got enough to call yourself S.M.A.R.T. Let me show you why. Instead of saying, "My goal is to lose weight," I can say to you, "My goal is to lose thirty pounds in thirty days." Not only can you measure whether or not I have succeeded at thirty days, but you can also look at the number of pounds I've lost. If I lost twenty-six pounds, I got six-sevenths of the way there. That's pretty good!

Allow me to share with you some specific S.M.A.R.T. goals for smoking. If I haven't given you enough examples by now, here's a final set to help you dial into your first smart goal.

1. Quit smoking within ninety days.
2. Switch to 50 percent vaping within thirty days.
3. Switch to 100 percent vaping within sixty days.

4. Change from reds to lights before Christmas.

5. Cut my spending on cigarettes by $100 a month.

What I want you to see here is that now we're going to bring in some of those different methodologies so that we have measurable goals. The cool thing is that just like you habit-stack, you can goal-stack. Once you finish and achieve one goal, you're ready to go for the next one. You may find that you need to use some of those other techniques, whether it's group support or vaping, to bridge yourself.

Your first initial goal will be to quit smoking using one of these tools, then the second goal that you stack behind it will be to remove the need for that tool. If you replace smoking with vaping, you can still get to the point where you also remove vaping from your life.

Let's get in full control, shall we?

Reflection Questions

1. Have goals in the past failed?

2. Why do you make malleable goals?

3. Are you hedging your bets from day one?

4. Do you think getting more detailed with S.M.A.R.T. goals will lead to more success?

5. Are you hesitant to set specific S.M.A.R.T. goals because you're afraid to look in the mirror if you don't hit them?

6. Are you willing to stay with me on this journey and fight for the life you deserve?

Your Action Plan

Your mission right now is to lock in your clear overall goal. What is your big picture and time frame? Implement everything from this chapter. Write down your answers in your journal, and then go beyond that. Take your goal and slice it into pieces.

If your goal is to go from thirty cigarettes a day to zero in thirty days, take a calendar and write down how many cigarettes you're allowed to have each day for the next thirty, twenty-nine, twenty-eight, and so on.

Write down your final goal on your calendar so you can see when you're on track each day. Again, I encourage you to share it with others in a community or on Facebook, so we can support you, encourage you and check in with you to see if you're on track for your goal.

STEP 3

Turn a Goal into a Habit

Success doesn't happen in a single day, especially with powerful habits, whether we're building or stopping. It's a process, and a key component to that process is to create one habit at a time. We want to start by quantifying our habits and breaking down our process into small and manageable bites. We want to focus on replacing each of our triggers and negative habits, with positive ones. We start one at a time, and stack them on top of each other.

If your most powerful trigger is for a cigarette first thing in the morning, then we want to replace that until you can consistently start every day with the right habit. It eventually becomes ingrained in you. Then we add the second habit and the third. For example, every time you feel the desire to light a cigarette after lunch, you can go for a walk instead. We want to start with small and manageable chunks because this is how the brain gets rewired.

Starting with your goal in mind is good, but once you start working through those habits, you may discover that you need to adjust one way or the other. This is where the R in the S.M.A.R.T. goals comes from: Reasonable. Your level of physical addiction, the power of your motivation, the stresses and triggers in your life, how many cigarettes you smoke a day—all of these will affect how quickly you can put everything down.

For some people, cold turkey works; for others, it simply doesn't. You may find that at first, you can't even quit a single cigarette a day. You might be locked into thirty cigarettes a day for the first month of this process, while you build in other healthy habits throughout the day. When you add in walking, biking, or eating a little bit healthier, it causes your body to shift your mindset, and then going from thirty to twenty cigarettes a day becomes easier.

Quitting smoking doesn't have to start with putting down that first cigarette. This process is about adding in positive habits, and each time you add in a healthy habit, it pushes the unhealthy habits a little further away. That's the beauty and the power of effective habit stacking.

At the end of the first month, as you're getting into this process, you may discover that you need more time, that there are certain triggers you weren't ready for, or that another stressor enters your life. You might have to adjust as you go.

Measuring *Your* Success

Even if you quit cold turkey, the process is not finished after a single day. Quitting cigarettes is not a moment. It's a journey. I haven't smoked in a very long time, but it doesn't mean I'm done. I have people in my family who've been through the AA program and struggled through that process. There's a reason why everyone starts by saying how many days they've been sober. It's a process.

Nicotine and tobacco are very powerful chemicals, and the addiction can crawl back if you make the mistake of saying, "OK, I've quit smoking, I'm done. I don't need to do these positive habits anymore."

We must stay vigilant, and that's why instead of just quitting smoking, we're filling your life with a series of positive, powerful, effective, healthier habits and building a new lifestyle.

It's a stressful period for me. Ten minutes ago, I was lying on my bed, thinking about just going to sleep. I thought to myself, *You know what? I don't feel like doing it. I'm a little bit stressed.* As much as I've written multiple books on it, depression is still a powerful force. I know that if I lie down and try and go to sleep during the day, that's a sign of depression and a negative trigger. I don't need to sleep in the middle of the day.

I fought that trigger and went outside. I started my ritual of getting my backpack ready and organizing everything to come outside and spend time writing this book. I went through that process and began a positive habit trigger. I felt exhausted just fifteen minutes ago, and now I feel fully energized. Even though I haven't had a major depression strike in over two decades, I felt it trying to creep in. Overcoming depression and quitting smoking are both processes that I experienced deeply in my life. I am still defeating depression; having that mindset is critical so that you don't slip up in a year or two.

People often misperceive success, and they think it happens overnight. When we look at billionaires, we often ignore the fact that they spent ten years programming computers while living in a basement or spending the night in a sleeping bag underneath their desk. The problem is that this mindset affects our self-perception. If you think quitting smoking was easy for me, and then you go through this process and it takes you time, you will get down on yourself. That's why I'm warning you here.

Success is a process. It's the grind and the effort, the wins and the losses. The real journey is about staying the course. Every single day that you go without having a cigarette or bring yourself one step closer to your goal, that's a massive win. This is important to dial into. One of the best things about breaking our big goals into smaller habits is that they give us multiple successes throughout the day, and you can reward yourself.

Each time you succeed with the habit, you are going to be proud of yourself. Every time you go past one of your usual triggers, every time you have a meal without smoking, every time you don't take a smoke break, you can look in the mirror and say, "You did it. That's a win." Rather than experiencing just one success a day, you can experience dozens, and that will keep you in a perpetually positive state.

This is how you can achieve massive success. You don't have highs and lows, and you are no longer riding an emotional roller-coaster. You're on a magic roller-coaster that only seems to go up. That's the beauty of this process. Focusing on smaller goals and giving yourself affirmation keeps you in an upswing state.

Thomas Jefferson once said, "I'm a great believer in luck. The harder I work, the more luck I have." The key to successful people is that they use small actions. They identify the critical steps and repeat them.

When you know the important tasks related to your goal and do them continuously, you'll surpass the folks who spend their time making excuses about why they're not successful.

To quote Jeff Olson, from his book *The Slight Edge*:

> *The truth is, what you do matters. What you do today matters. What you do every day matters. Successful people … do things that seem to make no difference at all in the act of doing them, and they do them over and over and over until the compound effect kicks in.*

That compound effect that Olson talks about can be achieved by introducing small actions into your daily life.

At first, you may feel an emotional dip as you're testing this process and experimenting because you don't have massive life-changing success. But you're building one brick at a time. Realize that you're on a journey and the small habits add up. Life is not made up of giant events. Instead, it's made up of the little pieces and decisions that lead you up to that moment.

Dr. Philip Zimbardo, one of the most notorious experimenters in all of psychology—the one who ran the famous Stanford prison experiment—to make up for how the experiment went bad, has spent thirty years researching what makes people into heroes.

In a brilliant TED Talk, he explains that heroes are not built in a moment. Instead, they're the result of a series of actions that lead to that moment. When someone falls under the subway tracks, the man who dives on top of them and saves them wasn't a hero an hour earlier, but he is a hero an hour later. In that moment, all the decisions he made leading up to that moment led him to be someone who would take action, while everyone else didn't have that within them.

It's not that we're fundamentally different. Sometimes, everything just comes together, and it's the series of right decisions made through small habits that will build you into someone very powerful. You'll become a person who lives a healthy life, and when you are that person, smoking becomes the exact opposite of what you'd ever do. I literally cannot imagine bringing smoking back into my life because I would have to undo so many other habits that I've built over the past five years.

As you move in the right direction, the series of positive things you add into your life are what will keep you from relapsing one, two, or twenty years from now. We're building a framework to protect and strengthen you, because you're still going to have stress in the future. You're still going to have tough days, and the temptation will arise.

Flexible Goals versus Brittle Goals

One of the biggest dangers when setting goals is to be too brittle. Perhaps you've heard the metaphor of the bendy tree versus the very stiff tree in the storm. The stiff tree resists until it cracks, and the bending tree bends, and when the storm ends, it flips back up to normal.

That's who you want to be.

You're going to make mistakes. You're going to slip up. You're going to have a temptation or a day when you have a cigarette because you forgot that you quit. Knowing that there's going to be a mistake will keep you from forming brittle rules.

When we form brittle goals, they become "yes or no." The problem with that is a single slip up turns into giving up. This is why most diets fail. We miss a trip to the gym. We miss a healthy meal. We eat something we shouldn't have, and that mistake shifts from being an aberration to being a new habit because we say to ourselves, "I've already failed, so I might as well ..."

For instance, if you have a goal that's too brittle, you might tell yourself: "I've already had a cigarette this morning. What difference is the second one going to make? I've already failed for the day."

That's why rather than measuring one day at a time, you should measure one cigarette at a time. Prepare for the reality that mistakes happen; you're human. I'm human. It took me a lot of quits to get my final quit. I had some really good ones along the way.

Biting Off Too Much

Sometimes we take on too big of a goal. If you've been smoking for fifty years, your struggle is going to be different than mine. But it's OK because we've pre-built in the ability to pivot and shift our goals to keep them realistic. It might take you a full year to quit. So what? A year from now, you're going to be awesome! It can be a process, as long as we continue to get healthier, decrease how much we smoke, and replace and improve our habits.

If we see it as a journey, then suddenly, it's not that big of a deal.

Instead of saying, "My journey will happen in a single day, one year from now," you're saying, "It's a journey of 365 steps, and I have already taken the first one. I'm already on the path to success." That's a difference in perspective, and it's what will help you to succeed.

Different Types of Goals

There are different types of daily goals and habits. You can establish yes/no goals, but you want to make them very clear.

Like: "Did I walk today?" Yes or no.

Or: "Did I smoke today?" Yes or no.

It's even better when your goal is broken down into measurable pieces.

Like: "Did I walk five times today? Did I walk five miles today? Did I not smoke twenty cigarettes today? Today was a little bit rough. I smoked three cigarettes, but I didn't smoke the other seventeen."

It's much better to say, "I smoked seventeen out of twenty cigarettes" than to say "Yes, I smoked today." That's brittle. While it's measurable, it's binary and not realistic enough, because this process is a journey.

If you normally smoke thirty cigarettes a day, and you just smoke one, marking that day on the calendar as "day I smoked" is counterproductive. Just like there's a big difference between me going for a swim with my son in the pool, where I can stand and touch the bottom anytime, and me swimming five kilometers and measuring it with a stopwatch. Technically, I was swimming both times, but definitely not the same.

We want to be sure the way we measure our goals, habits, and successes is quantifiable, so that we can track everything in your journal. We can create a cool line graph moving through time, so that we can see success over time. If we oversimplify our measurements, then they become useless.

Practice Daily *Habit Stacking*

One trick to breaking the smoking habit is to ask yourself: "What can I do every day to reduce my number of cigarettes?"

The short answer is: you replace the triggers that prompt you to smoke with healthy habits.

But as you've probably experienced, it's not easy to build new habits. You already have many tasks in your life, with an ever-increasing list of obligations. It might seem impossible to add something new to your daily routine. It's my contention that not only do you have enough time to build a single new habit, but it's possible to add dozens of habits to your busy day without it negatively impacting your life.

All you need to do is:

1. Identify those small important actions (like taking a quick five-minute walk and preparing a nutritious smoothie)
2. Group them together into a routine with equally important actions.
3. Schedule a specific time each day to complete this routine.
4. Use a trigger as a reminder to complete this stack.
5. Make it super easy to get started.

In essence, the goal here is to complete the habits that you know are important by stacking them on top of one another.

This is a concept that Steve calls *Habit Stacking* in his book by the same name.

Habit stacking works because you eliminate the stress of adding too many new things to your life. You begin with a few simple but effective habits and then build on them as this routine becomes an important "can't miss" part of your day. This stack (and the others you build) will become as important as the routines you follow when you get up in the morning, prepare for work, and get ready to sleep.

We've been building up this process, and I've layered this explanation throughout the book: we're going to use multiple habits and layer them on top of each other to beat smoking. Some studies have found this concept works particularly well for smokers trying to quit the habit. When you use a gradual approach, it dramatically increases your odds of success.

Seven "Anti-Smoking" Habits

We want to build up a healthy series of habits that support your efforts to quit smoking—in essence, you will be attacking smoking from the side. We are going to focus on implementing healthy habits one after another until we've shifted to a healthier lifestyle. Your day will be so filled with healthy activities that you will decrease how many cigarettes you smoke without even trying because you're in a healthy mindset.

Smoking is a bad habit, but it's also a reaction to a trigger, such as lighting up when you're anxious, angry, or in uncomfortable social situations. Some people smoke when they're bored or while they're driving. The list of these tiny triggers is different for every smoker, but what we are going to do is replace our reaction to the trigger with a positive, healthy habit.

When you're anxious, take a walk. When you're angry, take ten deep breaths. When you have a list of tasks to be done, store them in your phone and knock them off one by one. Bring fruit or healthy snacks along in the car so you have something to put in your mouth to keep you going. Replace that negative habit with a positive one.

Part of the joy of smoking is the ritual—the whole process of buying a pack of cigarettes, pulling off the clear plastic, opening it up, pulling off the metal foil from the inside, flipping that one cigarette upside down, pulling out your favorite lighter, lighting up the particular way you like to do. All of that stuff is a series of steps that we enjoy as a ritual, and that's why a lot of the habits I'm about to share with you have those same elements.

#1: Make a smoothie. If you need a quick pick-me-up, instead of smoking a cigarette, try making an antioxidant smoothie. These delicious drinks contain essential vitamins and minerals, so drinking one in the morning can give you energy that will last for many hours.

There are a lot of smoothie recipes on the Internet, but I recommend mixing up different recipes that include proteins, fruits, vegetables, potassium, and antioxidants. If you're interested in some of Steve's favorites, you can check out the NutriLiving website and app (iOS and Android), which are part of the NutriBullet brand.

#2: Take a walk during your breaks. There is something about being stuck in a single building all day that just drains the soul. Perhaps it's the unnatural lighting or the line of cubicles. People aren't meant to be cooped up all day long. Every job, no matter how grueling, has breaks throughout the day. Rather than taking a cigarette break, go for a walk. Walking is one of the best ways to get regular exercise without negatively impacting your busy schedule. This habit doesn't fit neatly into a single stack. Instead, it should be completed throughout the day, usually after an intense block of work.

If you take a few minutes to get outdoors throughout the day, you'll get a regular dose of vitamin D from exposure to the UV rays, which our bodies need to function. There is increasing evidence that shows spending more time outdoors can reduce stress, combat depression, improve sleep, and have a positive effect on your well-being. In fact, a study published in *Environmental Science & Technology* found that just five minutes of exercise in a "green" environment led to mental and physical health improvements in the study's participants.

#3: Meditate. Meditation helps you maintain focus on one thing (such as your breathing or the sounds of the ocean) and block out any other distractions, including cravings. It has been proven to have numerous benefits, including reduced stress, improved creativity, better focus, and improved memory. Some people meditate for hours on end, while others just take a few minutes out of their morning. I suggest you start by meditating for five minutes, so it fits neatly into a habit stack. But if you start to enjoy it, then I recommend increasing the length of your sessions.

Here's a quick breakdown on how to meditate:

- Find a quiet place that's free from distractions and set a timer for five minutes.

- Start by taking a deep breath and releasing the tension from your diaphragm.

- Stretch your muscles, so you stay comfortable while you focus inward.

- Focus on clearing your mind and thinking about the present moment. It's natural to experience frustration the first few times you meditate. If this happens to you, focus on your breathing and let your feelings of frustration dissipate.

- Focus on your body parts, so you know when the meditation starts to take hold.

If you have trouble focusing, then try the Calm or Headspace apps, which provide specific prompts that you can use to create a relaxed state of mind. (You can also try other mindfulness and meditation apps for your specific needs.)

#4: Color in a coloring book. Adult coloring books are in vogue now. Studies have shown that adults who spend just a few minutes coloring are more focused, relaxed, organized, and calm. The act of coloring can be therapeutic to anyone who regularly experiences stress in their lives.

Coloring books are backed by solid science, showing that coloring improves mental health, even for adults. Coloring has a few other benefits, such as:

- Reminding you of simpler times and temporarily returning you to younger, happier years.

- Increasing your focus and concentration. If you're having trouble with a difficult task, you can take a coloring break until you're ready to try again.

- Creating a relaxing flow state that's like other mindfulness and meditation habits.

Coloring books may not be for everyone, but if you often feel worn out at the end of the day and smoke a cigarette or two because you need to relax, then taking time to do a little coloring can become a better relaxing habit.

This is a straightforward process:

1. Go to Amazon to browse adult coloring books.

2. Buy a few that look fun or match your personality.

3. Purchase markers, crayons, or colored pencils.

4. Take frequent breaks when you're stressed for five to ten minutes of coloring.

You might not want to carry a coloring book everywhere, as you would with a book, but if you keep one on hand at home, it can be a fun way to reward yourself between tasks or whenever you feel the need to unwind.

#5: Watch an inspiring video. Motivation is fleeting. You might feel excited one moment but then experience a crash in emotion when something negative happens. Instead of smoking a cigarette because you're feeling down, one habit you can use to "reset" your motivation is to watch an inspiring video.

You have a few options with watching inspirational videos. TED Talks are inspiring lectures from the most visionary leaders of our time. They tend to be ten to twenty minutes in length, so you might need to commit to a longer habit or watch a single video over a few days. You can access these videos directly through the TED website, but they are also accessible on a mobile app (iTunes and Android) and through a video streaming service like Roku.

If TED Talks aren't your thing, you can also find inspirational videos on Upworthy or your favorite YouTube channel. Watching a good video will not only give you a boost of happiness to start your day, but it can also positively impact the way you look at the world because you're constantly introducing new ideas into your subconscious.

#6: Do an activity that makes you happy. While taking a few minutes of "me" time is always important, there are much better things you can do than smoking a cigarette or two. Spending a few minutes doing something that makes you happy can change your perspective and make you more pleasant for others to be around. There are a lot of habits you can do in five minutes or less.

Here are a few ideas to help you get started:

- Write in a journal
- Have a cup of tea/coffee and think about nothing at all
- Sit outside and feel the sunshine on your face
- Cuddle/play with a pet
- Read a few jokes and laugh a little
- Listen to a favorite song
- Dedicate five minutes to meditation
- Stop and smell the flowers, literally
- Eat a bite of chocolate
- Take a short walk, even if it's just around the hallways
- Get a quick massage
- Dance around the room like no one is watching
- Enjoy a piece of fresh fruit

- Read a few pages of fiction

Sure, some of these ideas might seem silly, but that's the point. When you take the time to unwind and not focus on your to-do list, you'll discover it's easy to add happiness to your life and relieve a little bit of stress.

#7: Squeeze a stress ball. According to a study published in *The Journal of At-Risk Issues,* students who squeezed a stress ball throughout the day had a decrease in their frequency of distraction and an increase in their attention span, leading to better performance in school and greater personal satisfaction.

The act of squeezing a stress ball activates the hand and wrist muscles, and releasing the grip lets the muscles relax. Also, this repeated pattern alleviates tension and boosts blood circulation, which can help give you a quick afternoon pick-me-up. Stress balls are small enough that you can keep them on your desk or in your bag.

To properly use a stress ball, try these exercises:

- Squeeze the ball with your whole hand for a count of three before releasing. Repeat twenty times. Every time you release your muscles, your tension will be released along with your hand. Firmly pinch the ball between each finger individually and your thumb. Go through your fingers one by one on one hand and then switch to the other hand.

- Twist the stress ball around in one hand at a time. Alternate both the direction of the twisting and the hand to get the full benefits. These manipulations of the stress ball will help stimulate nerves in your hands that are connected to areas of the brain associated with your emotions. Activating these nerves work similarly to acupressure, where stimulation of one part of the body affects other areas of the body.

Time to Choose a Habit

It's time for you to choose the first habit you're going to bring into your life. Every time you feel stressed out, instead of lighting up a cigarette, try out a habit from this list. Start with the easiest one, and if it feels right, commit to doing it every single day. Once it gets ingrained, you will do it without thinking about it. When you wake up and go to make a smoothie instead of lighting up a cigarette, you'll know the habit is now part of you, and you can look to build the next habit.

Remember that the examples I give you are exactly that—just examples. In order for this process to work, you have to pick a habit that's right for you.

So now it's your turn.

If you haven't taken action yet, this is the time to do it. Postponing or thinking that you will start implementing the techniques in this book after you've finished reading it most likely means you will put this book down and forget about it.

We all make the common mistake of waiting for "the right time" to do something we know we have to do—be it quitting smoking, losing weight, or clearing up our desk.

In your imagined future, you will have boundless energy, eat a healthy diet, exercise on a regular basis, and work well into the evenings in order to get everything finished. However, the realistic "Future You" is tired, unmotivated, burned out, handling unruly children, and craving chocolate cake.

Stop waiting for the right time to quit smoking because the right time is *now*.

Reflection Questions

1. Which of the seven habits have you tried before?
2. Have any of these healthy habits worked in the past, and are you still implementing them, or have they faded away?
3. Why have some of your healthy habits in the past faded away or failed?
4. Are you excited to try some new simple habits?
5. Does it feel a lot easier for you to start this process by just making a healthy smoothie every morning for breakfast rather than trying to quit cold turkey?

Your Action Plan

Choose a habit from the list of seven anti-smoking habits and implement it for one week.

Record your ups and downs each day in your journal and assess yourself at the end of the week.

Track all your daily behaviors. Does the number of cigarettes you smoke each day shift after you start making your daily morning smoothie, or are you lighting up a cigarette while you make your smoothie?

Do you go for a walk every time you feel stressed out and half the time you light up a cigarette while you're walking?

Record and assess your progress on a daily basis so you can look back and see how far you've come after a week.

STEP 4

Create Your First Healthy Habit

Our body forms habits in two ways. We have a system for building new habits and one for stopping habits. We are going to call them the "start" and "quit" systems.

The start system is very strong. It's similar to the way you could program a computer with a macro, where you hit one button and a bunch of things happen. On the other hand, the stop system is very weak and brittle. Several studies have shown that it's about 10 percent as effective, which means that trying to quit a habit is ten times harder than trying to pick one up.

We're going to stick to what is more effective. Plus, it leads to you having better elements in your life. The quit system is very brittle because if you get stressed out, distracted, or even if you just have a couple of drinks, any habit you're trying to stop will collapse. **Our secret to success is that we're going to use habit replacement, the start system, instead of trying to quit.**

Quitting has failed in the past for many of us because we just removed a bad habit, and then there was this emptiness left in both our emotions and our time. Instead, every time we take away that bad habit, we're going to put something better in its placeso your schedule is always busy. Distraction can often be the solution to a negative habit, and that's why we're going to stay busy with powerful, positive habits that we're going to stack on top of each other.

The Mindset Trap

The reason we're starting with really small habits is that it's easy for you to fall into the "mindset trap." Most people tell themselves, "I'm quitting something I enjoy in order to get a long-term reward." This mindset fails nearly 100 percent of the time, and this is where you can get stuck. Finding your why is the beginning, but the second step is just as critical.

When you make this mindset mistake with every form of quitting, whether it's diets or quitting smoking, gambling, or drinking, you will always struggle. Your mind will be at war with itself because part of you wants to smoke, and part of you doesn't. And when a minority of your personality wants to do something, it will wait for the opportunity and eventually strike. You'll make a decision you later regret.

Instead, we're going to use the mindset that works. We're going to remove the desire to smoke, and then implementation becomes easy.

I suggest creating the following as your first habit:

Create a trigger where you frequently tell yourself that "smoking is gross."

You might not realize this truth right now, because you're the one who is smoking, but don't just take my word for it. Here is a story one of our readers has shared with us:

"I did everything to try and quit smoking, but what helped me to just quit for good was to visit a dating site. When I said I was a non-smoker, I received over 990 possible 'likes.' When I changed my profile to a smoker, I had four likes. That did it for me; I quit cold turkey. Now I hate the smell, and I would be another person who would never date a smoker."

If you can shift to this "smoking is gross" mindset, instead of quitting something you like, you're quitting something you find disgusting. We're short-circuiting the smoking habit by striking it before the habit triggers. It may take you time to complete this process, but when you master this habit, the rest of the process becomes inevitable.

Before we move on to the next chapter, I want to share with you a couple real-life stories that two members of our audience kindly shared with us. I'm sure you will be inspired by their words.

Here's the first story:

> *Not being sure enough that you want to stop always holds me back. If you reject smoking enough, you can finally stop. You have to genuinely associate it with bad enough things to override all the good, comforting, and creative associations. It was the thing that worked for me after decades of trying. It had to feel like the most serious threat to everything you want most. Then you can stop then and there.*

And here's the second:

> *What helped me to quit most was two things: my health and my rebellious spirit redirected. First, I began envisioning myself as a non-smoker—how great that would feel and how much time I would have. You will be amazed at how much more time you have when you don't smoke. It really steals your days, both time wise and health wise. Second, I redirected my rebellion toward the manufacturers of*

cigarettes. I was working hard for my money, and handing it over to them for the sole purpose of providing a product for my use that would kill me. Pretty dumb, huh? It made me angry at them, and I began envisioning the things I could do with my own hard-earned money rather than give it to those rich fat cats in return for my early death.

This is what this transaction with them is all about. Get mad, show them you don't need them, show them you won't let them harm you anymore. After all, if they came at you to do you immediate physical harm, you'd duck, right? Every time I see a person smoking, I see a dead man/woman walking, and I wish for a smoke-free world and penniless cigarette manufacturers!

Hopefully, these two stories will give you that subtle push to reframe how you view cigarettes and people who smoke.

Reflection Questions

1. Do you see how trying to quit something you want to do is hard?

2. Are you ready to get into mental alignment and stand firm against smoking?

3. Can you see why quitting smoking is easier when you remove the desire?

4. Is my secret to success starting to make sense to you, or does this sound ridiculous?

5. Is there a part of you that's still saying, "This might work for someone else, but it won't work for me?"

6. Are you willing to try habit forming?

Your Action Plan

This activity is critical—maybe the most important activity in the book. I want you to make a commitment to change your mindset before you work on anything else. I want you to shift into hating smoking, however you have to do it, and spend time vocalizing it because what we say and do begins to affect how we think.

Talk about how much you hate smoking. You could even go as far as using an app like Mind Jogger to send you random reminders telling you that *smoking is gross*.

STEP 5

Build the "Quit Smoking" Habit Stack

We're going to use the principle that Steve has developed and refined over the last five years as part of the habit stacking process. The core idea is that you start with something very small and then add on other habits.

As you've probably experienced, it's not easy to build new habits. You already have many tasks in your life, with an ever-increasing list of obligations, so it might seem impossible to add something new to your daily routine. It's my contention that not only do you have enough time to build a single new habit, but it's possible to add dozens of habits to your busy day without it negatively impacting your life.

All you need to do is:

1. Identify those small important actions.
2. Group them together into a routine with equally important actions.
3. Schedule a specific time each day to complete this routine.
4. Use a trigger as a reminder to complete this stack.
5. Make it super easy to get started.

In essence, the goal here is to complete the habits that you know are important by stacking them on top of one another.

You begin with a few simple but effective habits and then build on them as this routine becomes a regular part of your day. When creating a habit stack, you want to consider a few important elements:

- Why are you choosing each action?
- What order should they go in?
- And how long do you spend on each activity?

The key to consistency is to treat a habit stack like a single action instead of a series of individual tasks. I know this seems like a small thing, but building a habit requires many elements if you want it to stick, like:

1. Scheduling time for an activity (a block of time).
2. Identifying a trigger.
3. Planning what you'll do to complete the action.

So on and so forth.

My point here? If you treated each component of a stack as an individual action, then you'd have to create a reminder and track each behavior, which can quickly become overwhelming. However, if you treat the entire routine as just one habit, then it will be easier to remember and complete on a consistent basis.

There have been lots of recent studies on the power of building habits and how the structure works. A recent article in the *International Journal of Obesity* demonstrated that building a habit structure works if we approach a task by its component parts and then treat it as a series of steps. We want to look at building larger stacks as we push closer to success. Now that you've had some success trying out some healthy habits and understand that core first habit of finding smoking disgusting, it makes sense to build a longer series of habits.

You may need to approach this in a way that's unique for you. Everyone is different. For you, it might start with looking at how long a cigarette lasts. If a cigarette lasts eight minutes, you need a series of habits that last eight minutes, so every time you feel that trigger to smoke, you do something else that lasts the same amount of time. This way, a trigger caused by wanting to break up your workday won't lead you to smoking because you have replaced it with a better habit that fits into that same slot.

Another article from *JAMA Pediatrics* shows that routines are simply the result of healthy habits and long-term results. That's all that healthy children are. When you look at a child who is slim and strong versus a child who is overweight and slow, it's often a series of habits that makes the difference.

This is how we can move in another direction. Think about negative habits in the same way. Vices compound. Think about all the bad things most people get involved in; they're usually combined. People go drinking and then start smoking. Negative habits stack, just like positive habits do.

One of my favorite recent studies from the *Journal of Economic Behavior & Organization* found that believing you have the power to change your life is enough to give you the power to change your life. That's it. If you read this book, but you're thinking of all the reasons why this worked for me but won't work for you, that will hold you back. Once you realize you have the ability to change every aspect of your life, you become limitless. Stop saying you don't have the power to quit, because you do. The power is in your hands. I don't have the power to change you. I only have the power to show you the steps you have to take to make the impossible become inevitable.

The key to habit successes is repetition. Another study found that building a habit takes time, and repetition is the core requisite to permanence.

A habit is simply an automatic behavior triggered by a situational cue, almost without conscious thought. It's something we do without really thinking about it. A great example of a habit is how we check our phones all the time. You could even test how habits work by taking the battery out of your phone or letting the charge die and keeping your phone in your pocket throughout the day. See how many times you still check it. That's how we recognize an unconscious habit, and smoking is a very common and powerful unconscious habit. We often do it without thinking about what we're doing. We don't go through a decision-making or contemplation process, and that's the second place where we're going to slip into your decision-making loop.

We're not binary. According to research in the *Journal of Consulting and Clinical Psychology*, we're more than just either smoker or non-smoker. There's a spectrum, and a key part of a person's success to becoming a non-smoker is to add in a contemplation phase. What I would like you to do is every time you're about to light up a cigarette, have a conversation with yourself.

Ask yourself, "Why am I having a cigarette? Do I need the cigarette? Is it worth the negative results?" This is a great place to insert, "Cigarettes are gross. Why do I want to smoke this?"

Questions like these are the key to quitting.

Adding in the contemplation phase where we think about what we're about to do increases the likelihood that we'll make a healthier or better decision. While we're stacking positive habits, we also want to build in structure to put a barrier between us and a bad habit. I mentioned earlier how I don't keep snacks in the house. That is a physical manifestation of this principle. Walking from my front door to a snack shop takes less than thirty seconds, and yet I never go over there. That's because there is a contemplation phase.

While I'm walking there, I have to think about it. I think about what I'm doing and whether I'm making the right decision, and often, I'll just stop at the fridge on the way downstairs and get myself a glass of water with ice. We can use science to combat our smoking habit in the same way. Stop keeping cigarettes in your pocket. Push back on the convenience factor to increase the amount of time you spend contemplating whether or not you're making the right decision.

Six Steps to Build an Anti-Smoking Habit Stack

Now we want to begin a framework within your life to help you continually add and build positive habits. Some of the things I could say here would be quite obvious, like if you want to quit smoking, don't spend time around people who smoke. Instead, we want to start spending time around people who live the life that we want to live. Spend time around people who've already quit smoking or who don't smoke, and it will be far easier to stay the course.

We want a framework in our day-to-day life that is conducive to good habits. Part of our nature as humans is that we're social creatures, and we like to go along with what everyone else is doing. If you surround yourself with people who live a healthy lifestyle, the look on their faces when you try to light up a cigarette will make you never want to do it again.

Here is a six-step process that can help introduce positive habits into your life.

#1: Focus on one new habit at a time.

Don't try to include too much into your already busy life because you'll probably quit when everything gets too difficult to manage. Commit to each of the habits you're building for at least the next thirty days. You may have to stop and just focus on the first habit—finding smoking disgusting.

#2: Create a habit stacking trigger.

Next, we want to work on your "triggers," which are reminders that initiate the behavior. When I was really addicted to smoking, if I was reading a book and a character smoked a cigarette, I felt a craving immediately. Even when I was transitioning from smoking to non-smoking, even though I thought smoking was gross, that craving was still there. It was a process to fully shift to thinking that smoking is disgusting.

The word "trigger" has a different meaning for many people. *Our definition of a trigger* is a cue that uses one of your five senses (sight, sound, smell, touch, or taste), which acts as a reminder to complete a specific action.

Triggers are important because most people can't remember a large number of tasks without a reminder. So, a trigger can push you into taking action. For instance, many people use their alarm clocks or cell phones as a trigger to wake them up in the morning.

Here are four ways we suggest using triggers to remember the habits you'd like to build:

1. A trigger should be an existing habit. This is an action you do automatically every day, like showering, brushing your teeth, checking your phone, going to the refrigerator, or sitting down at your desk. This is important because you need to be 100% certain that you won't miss a reminder.

2. A trigger can be a specific time of day. The reminder for a habit can also happen at a specific time each day, like waking up in the morning, eating lunch, or walking through the door after work. Again, whatever you choose should be an automatic behavior.

3. A trigger should be easy to complete. If an action is challenging (even if it's something you do daily), then you decrease the effectiveness of the trigger. For instance, even if you exercise regularly, it's a mistake to use it as a trigger because you might occasionally miss a day.

4. A trigger shouldn't be a new habit. It takes anywhere from twenty-one to sixty-six days to create a permanent habit. Sometimes it's even longer for the ones that are really challenging. So, you shouldn't pick a new habit as a trigger because you're not 100% certain that it'll become a consistent action.

One great way to use triggers to your advantage is to anchor your new habit to an established habit. An example of this is to say, "After I get to my car from work, I will change into my workout clothes and walk for ten minutes." "After brushing my teeth at night, I'll write down how many cigarettes I smoked for the day." "After I drop off the kids with the babysitter, I will stop by the gym for my yoga class." These are all ways that we can attach something we already do to a positive habit.

#3: Identify your common pitfalls.

This means: isolate your smoking triggers, remove the triggers you can, and attach the trigger to a new habit.

For instance, two of my big quit failures were because I was around people who wouldn't stop smoking. As soon as I stopped hanging out with people who smoked, that trigger was gone.

One thing you're going to discover during this process is that I didn't cover everything or that you missed something during your one-day quit. I guarantee you there are triggers you didn't realize, and you won't realize it until you've been in this process for a while. I had no idea that reading a book where characters smoke would make me want to smoke even more. I couldn't even see the cigarette or smell the smoke, but just reading about it was a powerful trigger for me.

As you work your way through this, you'll find new triggers, and you'll have to find new ways to replace or remove them. I want you to keep track in your journal. When you identify your triggers, next to each trigger, write down how you're going to remove it or what activity you could replace it with. Every time you feel a desire to smoke, you can go back to that page and say, "No, this is what I'm supposed to do. I have an instruction manual right here." It's a very effective tool that'll help you to push back and turn off those triggers.

#4: Design your environment for success.

We want to design support habits that make everything else easier. When you surround yourself with habits that make the other habits easier, it's more likely to happen.

For example, one of the number one reasons I will not work out is that my gym clothes aren't clean. I can build other habits to prevent that from happening, which means either buying extra exercise clothes or building in a support habit for how to handle my laundry.

Another example is stopping at a gas station. Keep healthy snacks in your car so you don't have to stop at a gas station. You don't want to stop to get your snacks there; that's where they sell cigarettes. Surround your life with the framework of a healthy lifestyle. Make it easier for to do the right thing and harder to do the wrong thing.

If you still have to keep some cigarettes around because you're not ready to get rid of them completely, keep the pack behind an apple. Every time you want a cigarette, you have to move an apple out of the way, and that will make you think, *Maybe I could just eat that apple.* Or if you're going to try and transition through vaping, keep your vaping rig right in front of the cigarettes.

Put a positive habit right in front of a negative habit to trigger a decision-making process.

#5: Take baby steps along the way.

Start with habits that are stupidly simple to accomplish and create a micro-commitment that is impossible to fail. It's more important to stay consistent and not miss a day than it is to hit a specific milestone.

You'll find that when you have a low level of commitment, you'll be more likely to get started.

You can zero in on a micro-commitment such as:

- Walking for just five minutes a day
- Stretching for five minutes each morning
- Eating one serving of fruits and vegetables each day
- Tracking the food you eat daily
- Waking up each morning ten minutes earlier

Keep adding these small habits to your habit stacking routine until you have a solid thirty minutes of actions that will ultimately replace your smoking habit.

#6: Reward yourself.

Completing your habit stacking routine is an accomplishment, and it should be rewarded as such. Giving yourself a reward can be a great motivator to complete a daily routine. This can include anything, like watching your favorite TV show, eating a healthy snack, or even relaxing for a few minutes.

Really, a reward can be anything that you frequently enjoy. My only piece of advice is to avoid any reward that undermines the benefit of a specific habit. If you've just completed small actions to lose weight, then your reward shouldn't be a 400-calorie cupcake. It defeats the purpose of the stack, doesn't it? If you'd like more ideas, then I encourage you to read Steve's blog post that covers 155 ways to reward yourself.

Smoke Free: The Quit-Smoking Tool

All of these little steps will serve to shift your daily mindset and show you that you can build a series of positive habits. There is an amazing tool called Smoke Free that can help you with this process. It's available both for iOS and Android.

I spent a lot of time checking out many different tools. What I like about this app is, first of all, it's free. It does have an upgrade option that's a couple of dollars, but the free version is enough to get you started. The pro version costs less than a pack of smokes anyway.

Alternatively, you can use your journal or a small notepad. Just write down your daily successes, trials, and tribulations, and keep track of progress. Write down how many times you've smoked, where you found a new trigger or a new challenge that you've previously never encountered. This will help you to reaffirm your successes, to reassess when necessary, and to learn from your mistakes.

The benefit of having an app like this on your phone or having a pocket-size journal is that it's always with you. The phone app is amazing because it's filled with useful metrics. Not only does it track your health, but it also tracks how much money you've saved and gives you micro-rewards, "Hey, you saved $7 today!" This success gives you little rush of dopamine and affirms your new habits.

Reflection Questions

1. Have you thought about your smoking triggers?

2. What happens when you're on a long flight or in a movie?

3. Can you go longer than you thought without smoking?

4. Have you been in a situation where you don't have access to cigarettes for longer than you expected? What happens? Are you able to endure the cravings longer than you thought?

5. Is this structure starting to solidify now, and is the order of this book starting to make sense?

Your Action Plan

For this activity, I want you to first download the Smoke Free app or get a pocket-size journal. Either way, find something mobile that you carry with you to keep track of your efforts to quit smoking.

Continue to track your triggers. Go back to your list, and if you haven't created one already, make it now. You need to have a list of every single one of your triggers and what you're going to do when it happens, because if you've made that decision in advance, you can look at your phone and go, "Oh no, this is what I'll do instead." You've prepared in advance. It makes it so much easier; rather than having to think of something to do when you have that trigger, you just have to go do it. It simplifies that process.

STEP 6

Create Accountability for Your Habit

One of the biggest lessons that Steve has taught me is that one of the keys to successful habit development is to add *accountability* for every major goal.

It's not enough to make a personal commitment. The big things in life require a solid action plan and a support network to tap into whenever you encounter an obstacle. This is true for your career trajectory *and* your personal development. When you have someone to cheer on your successes (or kick you in the butt when you're slacking), you're less likely to give up.

There are a variety of ways to be accountable, like posting your progress on social media accounts or telling the people in your life about your new routine, but I have found that there are three strategies that get the best results.

#1: Self-accountability. This is where your tracking apps come into play. There are some amazing apps you can use to track all your habits and hold yourself accountable. I recommend these three in particular:

- StridesApp.com
- Coach.me
- HabitHub

Everybody uses self-accountability. These are more general-purpose apps you can use on a computer, tablet, or phone.

The Smoke Free app we talked about earlier is most effective for dealing with smoking specifically, but all the above three apps can be really good if you're on a journey and continue to add more to your process—especially in this phase, when you're focused on adding in other healthy habits like exercising more, eating better, and reversing your triggers.

You can also create habit reminders to do your habit using calendar alerts or Post-it Notes. You can even put alerts on your phone to remind you when you're supposed to do particular activities at specific times. These apps and tools are very powerful in helping you to add new habits to your daily routine.

#2: In-person accountability. This is one of the greatest ways to form accountability for exercising. You have a buddy that you do everything with. In the Navy SEALs, no matter what you do, you have a partner for every single mission. Because you have someone you can rely on, you feel like you're there with someone else every step of the way.

The danger of choosing a buddy who's trying to accomplish the same goal as you is that if one of you stumbles, you can bring the other down with you. To avoid this, build a plan for exactly what you're going to do if that buddy falls so that you don't fall with them.

Alternatively, you can just have a spouse, a personal friend, or an accountability partner—someone who just checks in with you to see how your process is going. You can be part of a team or a class, or you can reach out to a coach. There are plenty of people who make a living by supporting and encouraging other people on the path to improving their habits and hitting their goals.

#3: Online accountability. Online accountability is a great way to check in and get quick feedback. We have that within our Facebook group: http://www.HabitsGroup.com.

You can also find online accountability partners and coaches. We've done our best to provide an environment where people can reach out, communicate, and give each other online support. If you have questions about shifting your goals or what to do if you stumble, having a bit of online support can make a big difference and help you stay the course.

Focus on Consistency

When dealing with accountability, you want to focus on consistency. It's more important to succeed daily, and that's why we want to start with small goals and habits, so we get used to succeeding. If you get used to a pattern of success, this process will become easier every day.

Quitting smoking is a war, not a battle. It's something that happens over time, not in a moment, so going in with the right strategy will help you when you have small slipups and tough days. Even if you slip up and smoke today, it doesn't mean you have to smoke tomorrow. When we're dealing with accountability partners, we often make the mistake of not telling them when we slip up.

I can tell you that one of the greatest ways to succeed is to immediately tell the people supporting you when you fail. That way, a tiny little mistake becomes nothing more than that, rather than a wound that festers. Your accountability buddy is not there to judge you but to support you. The last thing you want to do is provide a foothold for desire or negative thoughts. You don't want to start thinking of yourself as a failure or someone who lies to your support network. Instead, you want to stick with this process. Be honest when you have a slipup.

Focus on continually pushing to replace pleasure with disgust in your mind.

Never Break the Chain

There are little habits you can implement as part of this process to help you stay consistent, such as only buying cigarettes from one store or a store that's far away, or throwing away one cigarette for each one that you smoke so you can really feel that struggle. Cigarettes are so expensive. Think about throwing one away every time you smoke. Now it's twice as expensive, and it shows that there's no value to what you're doing.

Additionally, as part of your first small habit stack, always go through a contemplation and decision-making process before you smoke. You can make a rule that you have to wait five minutes from when you think about it to when you do it or don't do it. That way, you have five entire minutes to fight against that desire and activate one of your positive triggers.

During the earlier part of this process, we can focus on just getting one win. Just go for a walk for one minute. Just take the stairs instead of the elevator. Any activity, no matter how small, can become a win. We're going to build those small habits into something big.

There is a story that goes back to the 1990s, when Jerry Seinfeld was exploding as one of the biggest TV stars. A young comedian who met

Seinfeld asked him, "How can I get good like you?" And he said, "I have a giant wall calendar. Every day that I write jokes and work on my comedy, I put a big X on that day on the calendar. And from then on, my only goal is to maintain that chain. I can look at the wall and see my victory."

This can be a very powerful approach for you too. Put a big poster on the wall, and every time you have a success, draw a big X on that wall. Build a chain of success. You can also use Strides, Coach.me, or HabitHub to track your success; they use the same chain idea.

Our main goal is to recognize that even when we have a day that's less than perfect, we want to maintain that chain of positive action. We don't want to have a complete break. You might have a day where you break down, or something tough happens. If you smoke a whole pack but you still go for that twenty-minute walk, that's a demonstration to yourself that you are maintaining your accountability and that you're not giving up the fight.

Reward Important Milestones

One of the most common mistakes people make is to reward themselves with something that's the exact opposite of what they're trying to achieve. "I did so great on my diet. I deserve a piece of cake." "I did great with not smoking today. I will reward myself with a cigarette." The reward defeats the purpose of the endeavor.

Instead, create rewards that are in alignment with your goal. There are lots of ways to do this, and there are many milestones you can track.

For example:

1. how much money you've saved

2. how much time you spent not smoking

3. the percent of your habit shift

Every time you move down 10 percent in the number of daily smokes, that's a big event. Every time you go down by three, you get to have another reward. The more you celebrate your successes, the more ways you've developed to celebrate, the more dopamine you receive, and the more you train yourself to enjoy the process of smoking less. The less you smoke, the better you feel.

There are several ways you can track and reward yourself:

1. You can create a token economy: every time you hit a goal, you give yourself a coupon or a piece of paper that has a value to you alone, and once you've earned forty coupons, you can turn that into something else from your rewards chart. You can put anything you want on the chart as long as it's something good for you.

2. You can simply have an entire list of awards in front of you, where you say, "Each time I hit this milestone, here's the reward." That way, you can look at it and know what's coming. Build up a chart that's very exciting.

3. Simply track the exact cost of cigarettes where you live and create tokens that are worth as much as a cigarette. Every time you hit a certain milestone, you can spend the equivalent of that money on something else. Or if you prefer, you can save it all up for the big reward, like a vacation.

You can also combine this with the habit and S.M.A.R.T. goal concept. For example, every single day you hit one of your larger goals, you put a rock or coin into a jar. This needs to be more than for every cigarette you don't smoke. For instance, every time you save $10, you put a rock in the jar. That way, you can actually watch the jar filling up, and that's another way to see a chain of success. It's a great visual tool for tracking your progress. When the jar is full, you can spend those tokens or reward yourself with something big and awesome.

Reflection Questions

1. What time of the day is easiest for you to form new habits?

2. What time of the day are your triggers the strongest, or what time do you most frequently slip up?

3. Do you have your biggest successes when you work out in the morning or in the evening?

4. Do you smoke first thing in the morning, or does the craving get stronger throughout the day?

5. When you quit in the past, what time of the day did you fail? When did you slip up?

6. During the one-day quit exercise earlier in this book, when was it the hardest for you to stay the course? When did you feel the worst temptations, or when did you slip up?

Your Action Plan

It's now time to go big or go home. For this activity, we're going to share your progress in a public way. First, make sure to download the Smoke Free app. then you'll be ready to continue. Please don't read the next chapter until you download it.

Next, you'll look at each of the habit building apps and pick one that is the right fit for you. Once you've selected how you're going to manage your accountability, go ahead and implement your strategy. Buy that big calendar and put it on the wall, or set a jar on your kitchen counter and prepare the stones.

Whatever your accountability process, make your first post in a community or on Facebook and share it. Tell people your story: "I've been smoking for this long. This is my struggle, and here's my first goal." When you've done that, I'll be waiting for you in the next chapter.

STEP 7

Do a Weekly Review

The simplest way to stay on course with your efforts to quit smoking is to schedule a weekly review. This means that once a week, at the same time every week, you have up to a thirty-minute session where you analyze all your habits and goals. Go through your journal and tracking tools to see your progress. We want to look for trends. When we look back at the week, we may notice, "Wow, I'm most likely to have a craving right after lunch." That's where your main focus will need to be, so the following week you can work harder to fight against that temptation.

You should look for your vulnerabilities, but you also want to celebrate your wins. Whether they're big or small, you can look back at the week and give yourself a reward. We want to build in as many different ways to reward you as possible so that you constantly feel good about this process.

Reflect on your mistakes and look for patterns to find any triggers that cause you the most stress and craving. Maybe your boss is driving you nuts at work, and you want to smoke at the end of the day more than any other time. Once you isolate those most dangerous patterns, then you can deal with them.

As you go through this process, you'll continually find new triggers. Being vigilant and working this plan will help you isolate, analyze, and overcome, so you can either replace those triggers with triggers for positive habits or remove those triggers from your life. If the same mistakes keep happening, ask yourself why. Is the goal too big? Are there other obstacles?

At the end of this weekly review, ask yourself three questions and write down the answers in your journal:

- What went right?

- What went wrong?

- How can I plan for next week?

Reflection Questions

1. Are you excited about building a weekly review into your week, or do you feel like you don't have enough time?

2. Is a weekly review something you would rather do by yourself or with a partner? Maybe it will be easier to do it over the phone or in person with your spouse or your accountability buddy, so you can work through the process together.

3. Is our strategy starting to click for you? Does it make sense now to continually look for your triggers and find ways to remove or replace them with healthy habits until suddenly, there are no triggers left?

4. Are you excited about this journey? Are you feeling more connected to your efforts to quit smoking?

Your Action Plan

First, decide how you're going to do your weekly review. You can create a page in your notebook that has your weekly review pattern—the questions you'll ask yourself, when you will do the weekly review, and how the process will work.

Write down your implementation process so that each week, instead of just looking at a blank page, you have everything ready in your notebook. You ask yourself a series of questions: How did I feel on Monday? What were my biggest wins and losses? How did I feel on Tuesday? What were my biggest wins and losses? Do I see any patterns or additional challenges that I didn't notice before? Are there things that changed in ways that were unexpected and I wasn't prepared for?

Block out a specific time every week when you're going to do your weekly review. I recommend you schedule a thirty-minute block on your calendar and set a reminder. Lock in that time and make it permanent. When you're ready, meet me in the next chapter.

STEP 8

Plan for Obstacles

When it comes to quitting smoking, you might experience some discomfort in the beginning. One thing you can do is become comfortable being uncomfortable. Mastering this skill can allow you to do pretty much anything. You can stop smoking, begin that exercise regimen, eat healthier, get that promotion, speak in public, and overcome specific challenges in your life.

Truthfully, most people choose to avoid being uncomfortable. Just the thought of working hard or experiencing some level of pain is the main reason they fail to change their habits.

For example, many people choose to live a sedentary life because exercising takes too much effort. It is easier to simply sit at a desk or lie on the couch all day. Now, exercise isn't torture; it's just something that takes some effort and a willingness to experience discomfort.

Similarly, when people try to push aside their junk food and start eating a healthy diet, they often discover that the new food on their plate is bland, unexciting, and not filling. Changing what your taste buds are used to is a bit uncomfortable, but to be honest, you can retrain your taste buds if you are willing to push through a little discomfort.

Discomfort is not a bad thing—it's just doing something that's not part of your normal routine. As people avoid discomfort, they pay the price of not being able to change things in their lives, not living a healthy life, and not being open to new adventures.

The important thing to remember here is that a little discomfort is healthy. It can actually turn something you perceive as dreadful into an enjoyable habit—if you're willing to push yourself at first. So, let's talk about how to do that.

How to Master Discomfort

If you choose to master discomfort, you can do it comfortably. While this may sound counterintuitive, it is possible; it means doing things at your own pace, a little bit at a time. If you're nervous about being uncomfortable and try to beat your nerves with an overly grueling activity, there is a good chance you will give up and return to what you are familiar with.

Here are five steps to success (as outlined by Leo Babauta in an article titled "Discomfort Zone: How to Master the Universe"):

1. **Choose an easy task.** Start with something small. If your goal is to increase your activity level, start with walking outside for thirty minutes a day. You already know how to walk, so this won't add any complications to something that you already do every day. Do not worry about your pace or how far you are able to go—just walk.

2. **Just do a little.** If you don't want to start with thirty minutes of something that you are not used to doing, start with five minutes. It doesn't matter where you choose to start, just make sure that you do.

3. **Gradually push yourself out of your comfort zone.** When you want to stop, push yourself just a bit further. Begin to sit through the moments of discomfort so you can get used to the feeling and see how it comes and goes. Each time you go back and try to do something, push through one more phase of discomfort to help you gradually learn how to comfortably leave your comfort zone.

4. **Pay attention to your discomfort.** Pay attention to your thoughts as you become uncomfortable. Do you start to have negative thoughts or complain silently? Do you start looking for a way out? How do your thoughts change if you stick with the discomfort and push your way through?

5. **Smile.** Learning how to smile while being uncomfortable can help you be happy with discomfort. Smiling sends a message to your brain that you are happy and everything is fine. It also sends the message to other people that you are confident in what you are doing, which will likely make you feel more comfortable as well.

Once you become comfortable with being uncomfortable, you'll build the mental willpower to implement any habits you like into your new life. Practicing discomfort is like building a muscle. If you work at accepting discomfort regularly, you'll realize that it isn't as bad as you think, and you will feel empowered and unstoppable.

Plan for Specific Obstacles

Every new habit will have obstacles. When you know in advance what your obstacles are, you can take preventive action to overcome them. So, in this section, I'll list some of those common obstacles people have. Many of these came from responses to a survey we sent out to our followers to get a wide perspective. You've already gone through the process of analyzing your own triggers, but some of these obstacles might be ones you haven't thought of yet. I want to give you a little bit of an edge and help you with the experience of our wider audience.

The danger of brittle goals is that they always break. When you assume that you'll never slip up or make a mistake, you run the risk of creating a negative thoughts cycle. You'll think to yourself, "OK, I promised I wouldn't smoke. I had a cigarette—I broke it. I'm just not able to quit smoking."

I don't want you to get trapped in that cycle again, so here are some of those common obstacles as reported in our readers' survey:

#1: A spouse or partner smokes

This is the biggest barrier to success, and it can be brutal. Only when I stopped hanging out with my friends who smoked was I finally able to break the shackles of my addiction. But if you have a spouse or partner who smokes, it's not that easy to remove that obstacle, so plan for that situation. Most people attempt to get their partner to quit with them, but if your desire and your partner's desire to quit are not equal, it won't work. They'll fail and bring you down because they don't want to quit as badly as you do.

Instead, you need to have a conversation with this person; make it clear that you're trying to quit and that they're one of the biggest barriers to your success. You need them to be on board with helping you quit. They can continue smoking, but they have to promise not to smoke in front of you, not to offer you cigarettes, not to tempt you. Explain that you want to do this because you want to live longer, you want to be healthy, and you want to spend more time with them and with your loved ones.

The last thing you want is to spend the rest of your life hating your partner because he or she became the reason you couldn't quit. Say that it would cause emotionally devastating damage to your relationship if they didn't support you in this important change. Make it clear that you're not trying to change them, but you need their support because you want to change your own life for the better. When they see how important it is to you, and when you speak of it in those terms, you will get the support you need.

#2: Peer pressure and social smokers

Here are some of the common struggles that our readers have shared with us:

"If someone smokes in front of me, or if I see a passing-by smoker, I feel that urge to smoke myself, too. This is what holds me back. When my friends tell me 'Let's smoke,' I can't refuse. I don't know why, but I can't say no."

"My partner is a heavy smoker, so there are always cigarettes around— and temptation. When I try to quit, he feels so bad and lonely with his addiction that he starts to unnerve me. I can't stand those fights, and voila! I'm smoking again to soothe my anger and sadness."

The best way to deal with social environments where you're used to smoking is to not be around them for a while. A common mistake people make when they're trying to break an addiction is to "test themselves" by going to a bar and trying not to have a drink or trying to have just one cigarette. I promise you that testing yourself or having "just one" never works. It always leads to failure.

Instead, as you're going through a transition phase, avoid these events as much as possible and develop alternate triggers—something that you'll do instead of smoking. Every time you feel that temptation, force yourself to go through that contemplation process. Maybe every time you're in a social situation and someone offers you a cigarette, go to the bathroom and do ten jumping jacks or ten squats. Something physical just to get your heart racing. You'll feel energetic and think, *Wait, I want to be in better condition, not worse.*

#3: Stress

There's a misperception that smoking is a stress reliever.

A few readers said the following:

"I think one of the main factors why I don't want to quit is that it's become a stress reliever for me."

"When I try to quit, I'm okay for a few days usually, but when I encounter a little stress, I go right back."

"The thing that always prevented me from quitting was feeling stressed out. I would get into a situation that was stressful and felt that I needed to smoke to cope. Then, when the stress died down, I was just a regular smoker."

It's a false belief. As we talked about very early in this book, on a chemical level, the measure of stress is blood pressure, and cigarettes increase your blood pressure and your stress. To deal with stress, either avoid the cause or stressors, or when that trigger comes in, have a new strategy in place to cope with it. It's a great time to sit down and meditate. Say to yourself, "I really want to have a cigarette. I'm stressed out right now. What I'm going to do is go somewhere private and meditate for five or ten minutes." This is especially effective if you meditate the length of time you would normally have a cigarette.

Use that technique to lower your stress, and if it doesn't work, then you'll give yourself a cigarette. Again, what we're doing is buying time and building in a buffer so that your stress levels lower, and you don't want that cigarette anymore.

#4: Boredom

"I smoke because of boredom. Even when I don't want to smoke at my usual times, I will because I don't have something to fill the space. When driving, for instance. Also, the hardest craving is right when I wake up. First thing in the morning my mind isn't focused just right, and I have to power through it."

"It's just inertia; it's second nature to light up when I am bored."

The answer to boredom is our entire, overall strategy to fill your life with healthy, time-consuming habits. Find a habit or a hobby you could just keep with you all the time so whenever you're feeling bored, you have something to do.

A great habit for combatting boredom is to keep an adult coloring book and some colored pencils in your bag or in your car. Coloring is so effective because it requires a significant amount of concentration, and at the end, you get the reward of having created a piece of art. I've designed some of these books, and I use them as a technique to fight against depression. They work wonders. If you're struggling with stress, coloring can be a great response to many of your smoking triggers.

#5: Pleasure

"I enjoy the taste, the action, and everything to do with the act of smoking."

"I have stopped smoking for ninety-eight days as of today. Prior to this, I often looked at smoking as a treat or something I deserved when I was stressed or even happy, which brought me back to smoking at every quit."

"Honestly, I enjoy it."

There are loads of different reasons to enjoy smoking—it looks cool, you like how it tastes or feels, or it's like an old familiar friend. This is why very early on we focused on changing our perspective on liking cigarettes to thinking they're gross. In this case, you have to go through a bit of a breakup. Sometimes, you're in a relationship with someone you have strong feelings for, but objectively, you know they're terrible for you. Smoking is like that: you're in that type of situation where there are some things you like about the relationship, but overall, it's toxic, and you need to let it go.

#6: The old number two

Only one person wrote this answer in our survey, but it's one that I'm very familiar with on a personal level. Smoking does make it easier for some people to go to the bathroom, but you'll find that just like you were able to use the bathroom before you started smoking, you can still do it afterward. This is mostly a misconception that is a result of your addiction. Your body makes you go to the bathroom at the same time every day. You may go through a period where things are a little unbalanced, but after a week or two, your body will get back into its normal rhythm, and this problem will disappear.

#7: My old friend

Here are some other reasons our followers have shared with us for not being able to quit smoking:

"Fear of missing something that belonged to my whole life."

"Insecurity; it's like having security a blanket."

"The soothing effect provided instantly by smoking."

"It's my crutch to focus."

"I don't smoke all day at work, and I look forward to a cig when I get home; it just generally makes me feel better."

"It's a way of feeling like I have company."

Sometimes, it's nice to have something familiar with you when you're in a new town or you're in a place where nobody knows you. You have something to keep your hands busy, something to make it look like you're not doing nothing. Again, we have to go through a breakup. We have to find new friends, and that's why we're replacing our old friend cigarettes with loads of new healthy habits that are good for us.

#8: Travel/commute

"My commute to work is the main trigger of my smoking. I live forty-five minutes away from my job so typically, I light up to keep awake."

This is similar to boredom because we don't have much to do while we travel. Sometimes, we just make smoking a part of our trip to work. It just becomes part of your daily routine.

Just bringing an apple or a healthy snack with you might give you something to do while you wait for the train or when you are stuck in traffic. We need to find a replacement trigger.

I also recommend you find a different commute to work. Take a different train or drive on a different road. This will help you to break the habit. Your overall habit is that your drive to work includes the smoking component, but if you drive in a different way, you break the overall habit, and then it's easier to break the rest of it.

#9: I'm a rebel

"I was a smoker many years ago. I was simply addicted to the habit. Nothing more. I felt like I was rebelling against what others wanted me to do."

I smoked to show everyone that I break the rules. I always knew smoking was bad for me, but I loved doing it because I liked being a bad boy. I wanted to be like James Dean. James Dean died when he was ten years younger than I am right now. He's no longer my role model. He lived fast. He died young. That's not what I want. Something tells me that while you might have been a rebel when you were younger, if you've gotten this far in the book, you're not driven by that desire anymore.

There are loads of things you can do to rebel that don't hurt you. Smoking hurts you and the people you care about. That's the *worst way* to rebel.

#10: Mood shift

"I quit smoking years ago, however, I now vape, and I'd like to quit that. What holds me back is the physical urge and the grumpiness that goes with quitting."

Some of us use smoking to respond to all of our different negative moods, whether it's stress, depression, anger, or when we're feeling overwhelmed. Anytime we have a mood, we have a cigarette to soothe ourselves. You can replace this with a five-minute meditation habit, so every time you feel off-center, you use something healthy to get back in balance.

#11: Weight gain

If you follow the pattern of this book, weight gain should not be a danger for you. The reason weight gain happens is that most people, when they quit smoking, either just quit or take prescription medications with powerful side effects. As part of that process, they still have cravings, and they replaced one craving with another.

Our approach to quitting does not leave empty holes where you used to smoke. Instead, we're filling every hole with replacement habits, and you'll find that quitting in this way will allow you to avoid significant weight gain. If a little weight gain appears, don't give up your quit because you're on a path to success. You're going to add more healthy activities, a better diet, better exercise, and smarter living, so that weight is going to disappear anyway.

#12. Fear of withdrawals

"My fear and anxiety that I won't be able to cope without smoking prevent me from quitting."

"I'm too worried about side effects."

"I'm afraid of the withdrawals that I might experience for giving up something I have done for the last thirty years."

Withdrawals can be a powerful force. I've been through withdrawals in my life, and I know they can be brutal. I was curled up on the floor and throwing up for days. Withdrawals are a combination of psychological and physical factors. Rather than trying to break them apart into pieces, we just have to know they can be a part of life, especially if you try and quit cold turkey. If you're dealing with a withdrawal issue, you can try switching to vaping and slowly wean yourself off that way.

Of course, then you have to follow with quitting vaping, which is fine, or you may need the help of some medications or prescriptions, or you might try using the patch to slowly wean yourself off the addiction, but don't let the fear of withdrawals hold you back. Withdrawals can be overcome and defeated; you can bypass them. Don't be afraid of things that don't exist yet. Just know that we have a strategy and that you can overcome them if they happen, but our strategy is designed to avoid them.

#13: Fear of failure

"I'm afraid of failing (again)."

"What will I do when I need to relax? What will I do when I need a break? What if I fail?"

Failing or having a cigarette is a moment in this journey. It doesn't define you. You aren't permanently a failure if you slip up. It's not about "Have you ever failed?" It's about "What have you done lately?" When you have those dips, just keep going. Suddenly, you'll look back over the last ninety days, and you'll see that you've done great eighty-eight days—you've only slipped up two days. That's not the description of a failure. When we measure and track our progress correctly, failure becomes impossible because success is inevitable.

#14: Alcohol

Our vices like to join each other. We have a couple of drinks, and suddenly we find ourselves smoking.

There are two ways you can deal with this particular issue. Number one, stop drinking for a while. Number two, only drink in places where you're not allowed to smoke.

#15: Depression

As much as I try to escape from depression, it appears in my books all the time, and here it appeared in some survey responses. If you are struggling with depression, I recommend you read a book, whether it's mine or someone else's, and develop a specific strategy. One of my favorite and easiest approaches is, again, bringing out a coloring book.

Depression is a thought. It requires you to think about being depressed. If you get distracted, you'll forget you're depressed, especially in the early phases. Fill up your mental bandwidth by coloring a picture. Pick a complicated page that requires all of your focus. When you finish that picture, you'll notice that you don't feel like smoking anymore and you forgot you were depressed. This is a powerful technique I've been using for two decades myself.

#16: Work break

"It gives me five minutes away from work and a chance to socialize with others."

Replace your smoking break with a healthy break. Just talk to your boss and say, "Look, throughout the day, I have this many smoke breaks. I'm quitting, but I want to have a health break instead. I'm going to walk for the exact same amount of time it normally takes me to smoke because I want to replace a bad habit with a healthy habit. That way I don't come into the office smelling gross anymore. I will be better and more efficient."

Your boss is going to say yes because it's illegal for them to discriminate against healthy people. Your boss can't say smokers can have breaks and non-smokers can't.

Practice "If ... Then" Planning

The key to all these obstacles is to prepare for them, because they're going to happen. That way, we won't be blindsided by them. This goes back to the idea of "if ... then" planning. You want to create an "if" statement for each of these triggers or obstacles. Say, "If this happens, then I'm going to do that." If you don't like my suggestions, write down your own, or modify them to specifically apply to you. Write them down in your journal.

Here are a few examples:

- "If a friend offers me a cigarette, I will go to the bathroom for five minutes before I decide."
- "If I check the weather and it's raining, then I will go to the gym rather than using the rain as a justification to not go for my daily walk."
- "If my smoking friends invite me out to a bar, I'll suggest an alternative health activity or come up with a reason for not going."
- "If I start to feel a flicker of depression, I'll pull out my coloring book and color for ten minutes, no matter what."

Create your set of "if ... then" statements now rather than in the moment.

When You Completely "Fall off the Wagon"

It's easy to fall off the habit wagon. You're consistent for a few weeks, but then your schedule is thrown into disarray because of a vacation, emergency, or holiday (like Thanksgiving or Christmas). Next thing you know, this small hiccup has turned into a situation where you smoke more than you planned. Even worse, you play the "blame game," where you use negative self-talk and get mad at yourself because you can't stick with a new habit.

Trust me: the scenario I just described happens to all of us. Fortunately, there are two simple strategies you can use to reignite your dedication to quitting smoking.

First, you need to forgive yourself. Understand that everyone slips up from time to time, and nobody is 100 percent perfect with their habits. Beating yourself up for smoking accomplishes nothing. Our advice: take responsibility for slipping up, but also forgive yourself. Honestly, it's not the end of the world.

Next, "get back on the horse" by recommitting to your anti-smoking efforts. The key here (as you probably guessed) is consistency.

Some of us are going to have major setbacks in this process. If you encounter a big stressor such as a death in the family or losing your job, you might get completely overwhelmed, and despite all the efforts you put in, you start smoking again. When that happens, **do not give up.** You're still quitting.

As long as quitting is part of your process, as long as you're still adding in healthy activities, you can continue with this journey. It's very important at this time to reconnect with your purpose. Go back into that chapter and delve into why you're quitting in the first place, why it's so important to you. Connecting with that core principle will help you get back to quitting faster. Rather than spending a year smoking again, it'll just be a week or two, and then you can circle back to your efforts to quit.

Remind yourself why you want to quit so badly, and even though there might be a lot of guilt when you make a mistake, do not give up the fight. As long as you stay on this path with me, I will stay on this path with you. Even if it takes longer than you expected, as long as you stay on the journey, you *are* on the journey. Remember: quitting is a process, not an event, and you're doing a great job.

Reflection Questions

1. What happened when you failed in the past?

2. Does preparing for failure open up new hope for you?

3. Does setting up your first planning structure give you hope that this process can succeed?

4. Are you excited to implement these tactics and strategies to improve your success and help you quit faster?

Your Action Plan

What are your personal obstacles to success, and how are you most likely to fail? Are you ready to give yourself grace?

What I'd like you to do now is open your journal or notebook and write an entire action plan for when you fail. Prepare one plan for each of the different failures that we've discussed in this chapter.

How will you deal with it?

If you fail in a social situation or have a cigarette on the way to work, or you get stuck and really need a cigarette to go to the bathroom, whatever your failures are, we want to plan for how we're going to avoid them and what we'll do if it still happens anyway.

STEP 9

Maximize Those "Slivers of Time"

The real danger in your journey to quit smoking is knowing *what to do* when you have nothing to do. Boredom can strike while we're in between things, when we just have a few minutes available, and we can either fill them with positive habits or leave them as opportunities to stumble.

Boredom is a very common reason why we smoke. We're standing there waiting for a friend to arrive, or we're in between meetings, or in the car waiting for something to happen. Instead of allowing these slivers of time to be a vulnerability, we want to turn them into an asset.

Even if you only have a few minutes to work on something, I still recommend using it positively. We call these "short slivers of time," discussed by Suzanne Perez Tobias, and we can use them to make a little bit of progress toward an important goal that takes your mind off of smoking.

We can use this to focus on different types of habits. For gratitude, you can take a few minutes to appreciate the things in your life and your success in the battle against smoking. With mindfulness, you could meditate for five minutes whenever you're feeling a bit stressed. If you're focused on exercise, take two five-minute walks throughout the day, or even complete a high-intensity interval workout for just a five-minute block. If you're working on finance goals, you should be writing down your expenditures as they occur, so you can use a few moments to balance your checkbook and keep track of your finances throughout the day.

You can also build habits around random things that occur during the day, such as whenever you stop at a red light or a commercial comes on the television or a song ends. These little slivers of time that you have throughout your day might be moments right now where you're not smoking, but as we replace all of your normal smoking triggers, these can become new triggers. We don't want that to happen; to combat this, continue building out the "if … then" portion of your journal.

Building a "Quick Break" Stack

If you often have longer breaks, or if you simply like the idea of building a routine that helps you add as many healthy habits as possible to your week, you can create a "quick break" stack.

Your mind and body do require a break after working for a few hours. You could do what most people do during their lunchtime: eat, chat with friends, and browse the Internet. But a better use of this time is to grab a quick bite and practice a few habits that will provide an energy boost when you need it the most.

Here's an example of a forty-five-minute stack that is perfect for lunch break during your week:

- Get outside and practice mindful walking

- Practice progressive relaxation

- Clean your office desk

- Drink a calming beverage (like tea)
- Read a book chapter

Not only do these habits help you avoid smoking, they also provide a multitude of benefits to both your mental and physical wellbeing.

Reflection Questions

1. Is boredom one of your smoking triggers?

2. Do you have slivers of time throughout the day?

3. When you have five to ten minutes with nothing to do, is that time going to waste?

4. Would that time be more effective if you squeezed it all together? If instead of having multiple short slivers of time throughout the day you had a solid hour, would you use that time more effectively?

5. Can you see how focusing on our second level of defenses, moving past current triggers and looking at potential triggers, can protect you and create more of a bulwark against future smoking temptations?

Your Action Plan

If you haven't guessed it yet, for this activity, I want you to create a series of "if … then" statements in your journal. Jot down different events throughout the day where you have an opportunity to do something good.

Like:

- If I'm stopped at a red light …

- If I'm at a meeting early …

- If someone offers me a cigarette …

- If my favorite television show turns out to be a repeat …

- If my friends cancel plans …

When you identify your moments of weakness ahead of time (and have a game plan for handling them), then you'll be better equipped to respond in a manner that prevents you from lighting up. And keep adding these if-then statements to your journal. Whenever a new situation arises, write it down, and come up with a specific set of steps for how you'll respond.

Finally, focus on building healthy habits that you'll complete whenever you have those free slivers of time. Some of them occur daily, some occur weekly, and some only occur every once in a while. Creating these healthy habits means you'll never be vulnerable. If you find yourself with free time, you will be able to turn those slivers of time into positive habits.

STEP 10

Scale Up with Personal Challenges

Think back to the beginning of this process. Our initial habits are just five-minute routines, and our goal is to stack them until we have habits that are healthy and last from thirty to forty-five minutes. Our plan is to add a new routine every seven to ten days. The first week, you're just doing five-minute healthy habits. The second week, you're doing ten-minute healthy habits. The third week, you're beginning to move into fifteen-minute routine stacks.

At the same time, you're beginning to use these routines to replace and fight against your traditional smoking triggers. This scaling up doesn't mean you'll haphazardly add a bunch of small habits. Instead, you should make sure you're consistently completing the routine and not resisting this activity.

Pay attention to moments where you suddenly start to feel stressed, bored, or overwhelmed about your habit stack. If you notice that it's progressively getting harder to get started, you should reduce the number of habits and ask yourself why you want to skip a day. The more you understand your habit motivation, the easier it will be to overcome it.

Inspiring Stories

As we move toward the end of this book, I want to close out the story I shared at the beginning of the book …

When I was staring into that mirror, my skin was gray, my eyes were red and yellow, and there was blood in the sink. Looking between my reflection and my daughter's, at the terror in her eyes, I came to a revelation. I had been trying to quit smoking on and off for two or three years, and I realized in that moment that *this* was my final quit. If I quit and failed again, I wouldn't have it in me to try another time. This was my last effort. When I threw out my cigarettes that day and quit cold turkey, I was running away from death.

It's been years since I've even felt the temptation to have a cigarette. Instead, my life has grown healthier. I used to play with my daughter for twenty minutes, and then I'd be exhausted. I felt like a failure as a parent, but that's all gone now. Now I spend a lot of time with her, and we have a second child and a third on the way! I can feel my life extending now, compared to when I was a smoker at thirty. That's the most exciting part of my journey.

We mentioned an amazing guy named Leo Babauta a few chapters ago. He helped to develop the idea of mastering discomfort on his blog ZenHabits.net. His entire journey of self-discovery began when he quit smoking on November 18, 2005. It lit a fire that still burns brightly and taught him how to alter habits in a lasting way. Like many smokers, it took him multiple attempts to quit for good, but his success taught him how inspiring success can be. Each time you resist a smoking trigger, and each time you implement a healthy habit, that is a success. You can build a chain of success that leads to a life without cigarettes—forever.

My story of success is far from an aberration, and I encourage you to take a moment on the Internet and just do a search for the phrase "quit smoking stories." You'll find some amazing stories from people all around the world, and from celebrities like Jennifer Aniston, who was a chain-smoker for years before finally breaking the habit in 2007. She found that replacing her negative habit with a positive one and focusing on improving her body, especially with yoga and meditation, allowed her to stack positive habits, and she was finally able to kick her bad habit.

We found a variety of stories online, some were shared in this article, and from submissions by our readers.

Stories came in from regular people just like Terry, who spent twenty-six years smoking. Once she broke the physical nicotine addiction, she was then able to focus on breaking the mental addiction. When the desire was broken, she realized she could finally be free.

Leslie was desperate just three years ago. She hated being addicted to smoking, but she couldn't break free of the chains. She loved how it smelled, but she hated the damage it did to her. Like many of us, she was sick of other people telling her to quit. Eventually, she admitted to herself that she wanted to quit; she was tired of being trapped. You can convince yourself that smoking is critical to your happiness, that you love everything about it—from the rituals to the way it makes you feel—but when you quit, you suddenly discover that all that happiness you thought came from smoking was a lie. Nothing more than smoke and mirrors.

Nate started smoking in high school. Just like every other teenage boy, he wanted to be cool and fit in, but the habit lasted longer than he expected. He grabbed that tiger by the tail, and suddenly the tiger grabbed ahold of him. His throat was constantly swollen, and his doctor told him they needed to perform surgery to find out what was going on. He tried to quit smoking many times, but the cravings would always come back. Finally, the health consequences were staring him in the face, and he was forced to quit. After the first three weeks, things became a lot easier, and his smoking triggers weren't as overwhelming anymore. That was two years ago, and he no longer has a swollen throat. He no longer coughs in the morning.

Meet Adrian, who smoked for thirty years until he was diagnosed with kidney cancer. He found out that as a smoker, he was ten times more likely to get kidney cancer than if he didn't smoke. The next day, he quit using nicotine patches and relied on nasal spray instead. Two years later, he was still using that nasal spray and felt ridiculous. Unfortunately, he went straight back to cigarettes. It took him another four years to quit. His wife still smokes, and he's hoping that she'll join him. For him, life is amazing without cigarettes now, and he wants his wife to find the same happiness and health he's experiencing.

From Adrian's story, we can learn that sometimes we can get stuck on the techniques we use to help us quit, whether it's vaping, patches, nasal sprays, or gum. We eventually have to quit that measure as well. Sometimes, quitting doesn't work, and we end up smoking again, but Adrian never gave up and eventually broke the chains.

I want to share with you one more story with you…

Cuca has been free of smoking for seven years now. She felt like she was born smoking a cigarette, but after losing some of her friends to the many ways that cigarettes can kill, she realized she had to do something. Lasting change began the moment she surrounded herself with people who were encouraging her to quit and inspiring her in the same way that I hope her story inspires you. The first year after quitting, she depended upon a community—people who supported her and encouraged her journey.

That's exactly the type of community that Steve and I are building with the Facebook group I hope you joined. We want to encourage you and guide you on this path. After being free of smoking for seven years, Cuca has saved almost $15,000 and extended her lifetime by almost a full year; she's avoided over 75,000 cigarettes.

We all learn in different ways. We all need different types of motivation, and maybe these stories are exactly what you need to hear to push you over the edge. I hope they help you. It's possible to break free of smoking. I believe that.

I want to share with you something very special that Steve and I have been talking about. This book is not static; it's not written in stone. Instead, it's something living. What I'm looking forward to over the next months and years is to receive the stories that *you* share with us. We will add your stories to this book, so they can inspire someone else—just like somebody else's success stories inspired you and helped you to quit.

Scale Up Your Healthy Habits

It's important to celebrate your milestones and each time you trigger an alternate habit. You should celebrate each day of non-smoking, but I also want you to build in progressive fitness goals. Your first goal might be to walk up a flight of stairs without coughing. Your second goal could be to walk up the stairs without getting dizzy. Then you can graduate to walking up the stairs without breathing heavy, and then to walking up the stairs while maintaining your heart rate.

Set as many goals in front of you as possible. Choose different, little challenges. You can start small. Just start with, "I want to walk up a flight of stairs without getting dizzy," or, "I want to be able to run for ten seconds." If running is too much, start with, "I want to be able to walk for five minutes without my feet hurting." Start anywhere that doesn't feel too overwhelming, and then build up one little step at a time.

We can turn the stairs into ten or twenty smaller goals, and we get to celebrate each time we hit one. Keep pushing yourself each day. Stretch your goals by just 1 percent; that could be as simple as cutting your cigarettes down by one each day. Increase your healthy habits a little bit each day.

Keep Pushing Yourself

You want to continually push the boundaries and create more personal challenges that stretch you—do things that are hard but not impossible. For example, wake up every morning and exercise for five minutes instead of starting the day with a cigarette. Get creative. The more creative your goals and missions, the more you can accomplish.

One of the reasons I'm really excited about that Smoke Free app I shared with you is that it's filled with badges and missions, and gives you small daily tasks to accomplish. That's very effective because then you're focused on gaining points.

Build out daily challenges for yourself. You want to have a challenge that you know you can hit, a challenge you might be able to hit, and a challenge that'll be really tough but you're willing to push and stretch for. At the end of the day, smoking is a battle of inches.

Remember back to that first cigarette you ever had?

It made you cough and feel sick. You had to learn the habit of smoking. I couldn't remember how disgusting I thought my first cigarette was until I quit. Our body is telling us this is horrible, and yet we fight through it.

We're going to fight one cigarette at a time. Unlearning and breaking that habit and building a new habit is the same process. You didn't go from not smoking to smoking twenty cigarettes a day in a single day. Unlearning the habit will take time, and that's why this is a process. We're on this journey together. Remember that the more personal challenges you add in and the more you focus on the games and the rewards, the less you focus on the raw willpower struggle, which is the hardest way to stop smoking.

Reflection Questions

1. Can you see how making new challenges with a reward structure makes it easier to quit smoking because you focus on the game rather than the desire to smoke?

2. Can you come up with other fun challenges or successes you'd like to have?

3. Are you excited by how far you've gotten in this book and how much we've accomplished together—how close you are to the finish line in this moment?

4. Which of the success stories we shared earlier in this chapter most resonated with you?

5. How will you feel when you can share your non-smoking victory story in my next book?

Your Action Plan

It's time to create your own habit and goal stacks. You're going to write them in your journal, and also build out and implement the techniques we've talked about.

Write down a whole list of goals. Start with small ones, like being able to run down a flight of stairs without breathing heavier or feeling like you're going to throw up. Write that down and break it into smaller steps.

Create goals for other parts of your life or other ways you could find success. Let's say one of your goals is to take your money from cigarettes and go on vacation, but you realize the vacation is going to cost you more than a year's worth of smoking. You need to add in something to make a little extra money so that when you get through a year of not smoking, you can still go on that trip. Add in some additional challenges for new areas of your life.

Take the time to use your journal to write down as much as you can. The more you work with your journal the more likely you are to succeed. It's the people with the thick journals filled with notes, ideas, thoughts, and dreams that experience massive success; they're the ones who turn their lives. The people whose journals are blank or don't even exist are the ones who are least likely to succeed. A blank journal shows that, despite everything we've said in this book, those people have decided to fight in their minds instead of outside in the real world.

If you're having trouble thinking of challenges or you need more challenges, please make sure to join our Facebook group and communicate with other people. Ask them to share their goals with you. It's an awesome community. And at the end of the day, make sure you celebrate the wins.

Resources to Help You Quit Smoking

I want to provide you with a valuable list of resources you can use to learn more about dealing with the smoking habit directly. I recommend full immersion in this topic. The deeper you understand this topic, the better.

Knowledge is power. As Steve and I learned from the cartoon *G.I. Joe* when we were kids, "Knowing is half the battle!"

The earlier you can learn a harsh truth, the more time and opportunities you'll have to take action and make things right. If you don't like the idea of doing some research, ask yourself these important questions:

- What am I afraid of?
- Am I scared of the process or the result?
- Why am I putting this off?

There is a lot of valuable content out there that you can integrate with this book.

People learn in different ways. Some people need to hear, some need to read, and some need to see a video. That's why I want to provide you some high-quality resources that will help you to stay focused on the path of self-education. Everyone knows smoking is bad for you.

Everyone knows smoking affects your lungs and hurts your heart, but what else?

Don't assume that just because vaping is better than cigarettes, it's good for you. As we shared earlier in this book, there are some things about vaping that are not healthy. You're still putting nicotine into your body. You're inhaling chemicals that can actually turn into carcinogens.

Take a moment to look at these books, podcasts, videos, and articles and see which ones are the right fit for you.

Smoking Books

- *Stop Smoking Now* by Allen Carr
- *The Smoking Cure: How to Quit Smoking Without Feeling Like Sh*t* by Caroline Cranshaw

Healthy Living Books

- *Exercise Every Day* by S.J. Scott
- *10,000 Steps Blueprint* by S.J. Scott

Podcasts

- How to Make People Quit Smoking: A New Freakonomics Radio Podcast
- The Headspace Think Yourself Healthy podcasts: Stop Smoking
- Headspace Watch & Listen
- Spartan Up! - A Spartan Race for the Mind!

- The Fat-Burning Man Show by Abel James: The Future of Health & Performance
- Radio Headspace
- Half Size Me by Heather Robertson
- The Nutrition Diva's Quick and Dirty Tips for Eating Well and Feeling Fabulous

YouTube Videos

- What Happens When You Stop Smoking?
- This Is the Best Way to Quit Smoking
- What is the Single Best Thing You Can Do to Quit Smoking?
- Quitting Smoking Timeline
- How to Quit Smoking in 12 Hours the Easy Method
- Giving My Girlfriend $10,000 To Quit Smoking
- Extinguish ('The Easy Way to Stop Smoking' meets Brian Eno's 'Music for Airports')
- This Is What Happens When You Stop Smoking!
- How to Quit Smoking (FOREVER IN 10 MINUTES)
- How I Quit Smoking | Tips on How to Quit Smoking

Blog Posts/Articles

- I Quit Monday Blog
- The happy Quitter!
- Expert Advice Blog

- I Can Quit Stories and Experiences
- I Quit Smoking Blog Series by The Realistic Optimist
- The Ultimate Guide to Quit Smoking, Permanently.
- Trying to Quit Smoking? 11 Stop Smoking Tips from a Psychologist
- 5 Life Lessons You Only Learn Through Quitting Smoking

Reflection Questions

1. Is this the first stop smoking book you've ever read?

2. Have you immersed yourself in this knowledge and developed a deep understanding?

3. Can you see how becoming an expert in the dangers of smoking will help you when temptations arise?

4. Is there any critical piece of knowledge or information you feel was missing from this book?

5. Are you ready to go out and look at these other resources to continue growing and learning about how to finally quit smoking?

Your Action Plan

I want you to go through each of these links. If it's not easy for you to click all these, we have a whole Stop Smoking page, and every single link and book we reference is available on our website. We also have a pinned post to our Facebook group, so you can go to either place and get all the information.

For this activity, check out each of these books, articles, and podcasts and simply find the ones that resonate with you. Take the information you learned from these sources and delve deeper. Add notes to your journal so it becomes the ultimate bastion of knowledge.

Conclusion

We've reached the end of this book, and it's an exciting place, but I know that the end of this book is just the beginning of your journey. We've crossed a lot of bridges together, and I poured so much knowledge and inspiration into you that now it's time for you to take action, both in building positive habits and in pushing away negative ones.

I am going to give you a series of action steps you can take over the next thirty days to help you begin the process. The very first action step you need to take is so critical that it will significantly increase your odds of success: Join our Facebook group at HabitsGroup.com. You will instantly be surrounded by other people like you, and what's beautiful about this group is that there are people who quit years ago, people who are in the process of reading this book, and people who are just joining. You can inspire someone else with your stories and thoughts.

Surrounding yourself with people on the same journey is one of the critical keys to success. And we know that having the support of a community is one of the biggest indicators of success when it comes to breaking the smoking habit.

Here are the steps I want you to take to begin your journey to quit smoking:

1. Create a thirty-day action plan.

2. Set your first thirty-day goal. Where do you want to be exactly thirty days from now?

3. If somehow you haven't already, post that goal and the due date in our group so everyone can see.

4. Divide that into thirty daily goals so you know exactly how many steps there are between you and achieving that goal.

5. Break down each of your daily goals into as many tiny goals as possible.

6. Choose one positive habit from the ones listed in this book and focus on adding it to your life, whether it's eating an apple on the way to work or making a green smoothie first thing when you wake up. Focus on that for at least the next seven days.

7. Make a trigger alternative list. What are you going to do each time one of your smoking triggers rears its ugly head?

8. Implement that lists. Each time you feel one of your smoking triggers, you're going to use a positive trigger from the list instead.

Now, as I wrap things up, I want you to remember that quitting smoking is a dance. I've done my part; I've led. Now it's your turn to take the next few steps. If you enter the conversation with me, I can promise that as long as you'll stick with me, I'll stick with you.

Every time you email us, we'll reply. Every time you post in the Facebook group, a reply will be there for you. We'll support you, and continue to send you new content.

When you're struggling and even find yourself sitting there with a cigarette in your hand, send us an email. We'll do our best to get back to you as fast as we can. We will be there for you when you stumble or have a bad day, because at the end of the day, that's what this is about. It's about what we put back into the universe. Steve and I are dedicated to leaving the world a little bit better than we found it.

Thank you for being with me on this journey. I'm excited by everything that Steve and I have shared with you throughout this book. Nothing means more to me than changing lives.

So many people pick up books and don't make it to the end, but you did. Your journey is just beginning, and I can't wait to see how it turns out. I know that freedom from cigarettes is in front of you. It might not be there today. It might not be there tomorrow. But it's coming soon, and it's going to last for the rest of your life.

Thank you so much for reading this book, and I can't wait to see you on the other side.

Thank You!

Before you go, we'd like to say thank you for purchasing our book.

You could have picked from dozens of books on habit development, but you took a chance and got this one.

So, big thanks for downloading this book and reading all the way to the end.

Now we'd like to ask for a small favor. **Could you please take a minute or two and leave a review for this book on Amazon?**

This feedback will help us continue to write the kind of Kindle books that help you get results. And if you loved it, please let us know.

More Books by Jonathan Green

Serve No Master Series

- *Serve No Master*
- *Breaking Orbit*
- *20K a Day*
- *Control Your Fate*
- *Break Through* (coming soon)

Habit of Success Series

- *PROCRASTINATION*
- *Influence and Persuasion*
- *Overcome Depression*
- *Stop Worrying and Anxiety*
- *Love Yourself*
- *Conquer Stress*

Seven Secrets

- *Seven Networking Secrets for Jobseekers*

Biographies

- *The Fate of my Father*

Complex Adult Coloring Books

- *The Dinosaur Adult Coloring Book*
- *The Dog Adult Coloring Book*
- *The Celtic Adult Coloring Book*
- *The Outer Space Adult Coloring Book*

More Books by Steve

- *The Anti-Procrastination Habit: A Simple Guide to Mastering Difficult Tasks*

- *10-Minute Mindfulness: 71 Habits for Living in the Present Moment*

- *Habit Stacking: 127 Small Changes to Improve Your Health, Wealth, and Happiness*

- *Novice to Expert: 6 Steps to Learn Anything, Increase Your Knowledge, and Master New Skills*

- *Declutter Your Mind: How to Stop Worrying, Relieve Anxiety, and Eliminate Negative Thinking*

- *The Miracle Morning for Writers: How to Build a Writing Ritual That Increases Your Impact and Your Income*

- *10-Minute Declutter: The Stress-Free Habit for Simplifying Your Home*

- *The Accountability Manifesto: How Accountability Helps You Stick to Goals*

- *Confident You: An Introvert's Guide to Success in Life and Business*

- *Exercise Every Day: 32 Tactics for Building the Exercise Habit (Even If You Hate Working Out)*

- *The Daily Entrepreneur: 33 Success Habits for Small Business Owners, Freelancers and Aspiring 9-to-5 Escape Artists*

- *Master Evernote: The Unofficial Guide to Organizing Your Life with Evernote (Plus 75 Ideas for Getting Started)*

- *Bad Habits No More: 25 Steps to Break Any Bad Habit*

- *Habit Stacking: 97 Small Life Changes That Take Five Minutes or Less*

- *To-Do List Makeover: A Simple Guide to Getting the Important Things Done*

- *23 Anti-Procrastination Habits: How to Stop Being Lazy and Overcome Your Procrastination*

- *S.M.A.R.T. Goals Made Simple: 10 Steps to Master Your Personal and Career Goals*

- *Writing Habit Mastery: How to Write 2,000 Words a Day and Forever Cure Writer's Block*

- *Daily Inbox Zero: 9 Proven Steps to Eliminate Email Overload*

- *Wake Up Successful: How to Increase Your Energy and Achieve Any Goal with a Morning Routine*

- *10,000 Steps Blueprint: The Daily Walking Habit for Healthy Weight Loss and Lifelong Fitness*